Climbing
The Corporate
Ladder

Bud Bilanich
The Common Sense Guy

Other Books by Bud Bilanich

Career Success Books

Straight Talk for Success

Your Success GPS

42 Rules to Jumpstart Your Professional Success

Star Power: Common Sense Ideas for Life and Career Success

I Want YOU…To Succeed in Your Corporate Climb

The Art and Science of Success (contributor)

101 Great Ways to Advance Your Career (contributor)

Speaking of Success (contributor)

The Success Tweets Series

Success Tweets: 140 Bits of Common Sense Career Success Advice, All in 140 characters or Less

Success Tweets Explained: 140 Bits of Common Sense Career Success Advice Explained in Detail

Success Tweets for Finding a Job and Excelling in It (with Billie Sucher)

Success Tweets for Administrative Professionals (with Ketty Ortega and Chrissy Scivicque)

Success Tweets for Creating Positive Personal Impact (with Lydia Ramsey)

Success Tweets for Sales Professionals

Success Tweets for Speakers and Information Marketers (with Dave VanHoose and Dustin Mathews)

Leadership and Organization Effectiveness Books

4 Secrets of High Performing Organizations

Using Values to Turn Vision into Reality

Leading With Values

Fixing Performance Problems

Solving Performance Problems

Common Sense Ideas for Building a Dream Team

Supervisory Leadership

42 Rules for Creating WE (contributor)

Handbook of Leadership and Management (contributor)

Peace Tweets (contributor)

Praise for
Climbing The Corporate Ladder

"I've known Bud Bilanich for over 30 years. He provided me with great key organizational perspectives early in my career. He has continually refined his ideas on life and career success, and the result is a winner. *Climbing the Corporate Ladder* is a must read for anyone interested in moving up in a sure but steady manner."
   – *Tony Maddaluna, President, Pfizer Global Supply*

"Bud Bilanich is the real deal. He has a deep understanding of what it takes to succeed in your life and career. In *Climbing the Corporate Ladder* he presents his wisdom in his typical down-to-earth, common sense style. This is a book that you'll find yourself returning to again and again."
   – *Jack Davis, CEO Group DCA*

"Knowing and working with Bud, I have seen him put the principles from this book into action. *Climbing the Corporate Ladder* is a must read for anyone looking to advance and succeed in today's business environment. As you read it, you'll realize just how far common sense can take you."
   – *Lou Schmukler, President Technical Operations, Bristol Myers Squibb*

"There is a reason Bud is known as 'The Common Sense Guy.' His direct approach to climbing the corporate ladder is refreshingly honest and inspiring. Few career experts have the ability to make people not only see what they have to do, but act on it. Read this book if you want to finally get your career climbing in the right direction."
   – *JT O'Donnell, CEO Career HMO*

"*Climbing the Corporate Ladder* is a home run! Engaging and highly readable, the book is full of great ideas. It's a terrific tool for anyone interested in a successful life and career. These are simple but very powerful ideas."
  – *Ron Guziak, CEO/ President, Sun Health Services*

"This book is fundamental to your professional success. It applies to all business professionals and shares gems of advice that will both motivate and inspire you. Bud is a renowned career success expert. If you are serious about wanting to climb the corporate ladder, add this book to your 'must-read' list."
  – *Eric Harvey, CEO Walk the Talk Company*

"Bud has a down-to-earth, positive approach to helping you create your career success. He shares his ideas in a most engaging way. His wisdom comes packaged in an entertaining and uplifting presentation. You learn more than you realize because you're having so much fun along the way."
  – *Rich Smith, Vice President Human Resources Kaiser Permanente Northwest Region*

"Bud knows what it takes to succeed in corporate America. His pragmatic approach to helping you create your career success is simple and refreshing. Bud has found a way to condense his advice on a number of career success topics into a very usable daily approach. You can easily share this work with your entire organization to help develop future leaders. Outstanding!"
  – *Bill Piombino, Director of Operations, Lonza Biologics*

"No matter who you are, or where you are in your career, you will find hard hitting, pragmatic, useful common sense advice for success in this book. Read it and keep it near your desk for easy reference."
  – *Dana Ramsey, Vice President Operations, Childcare Network*

"In *Climbing the Corporate Ladder,* Bud Bilanich shares practical guidelines for corporate career success in an honest and entertaining format. This is the how-to book that lays it all out, and one you'll want to share with colleagues, friends and family. Full of wisdom and experience, this book should be in everyone's library."
  – *Betty Strickland, Chief Compliance Officer, Patriot Transportation*

"Bud Bilanich's 'Common Sense' column is one of the most popular monthly features in PM 360 because he provides brilliant advice on achieving success by employing simple, thoughtful, consistent practices. His common sense approach to career and life success shines though in his new book *Climbing the Corporate Ladder.* Bud makes common sense a science. You've got to read this book if you're serious about your professional success."
  – *Anna Stashower, CEO and Publisher PM 360 – the Full Spectrum of Product Management*

"Bud Bilanich is a personal inspiration for me. Positive, creative and a true example of success, Working with him was a time of personal and professional growth for me. I learned a number lessons that I continue to practice daily. I am thankful to Bud for being such a wonderful mentor and inspiration in my life. I recommend his new book highly. Buy multiple copies – one for yourself and several to give away. You'll want to share what you learn!"
  – *Jo Kelly Mohr, Regional Business Development Lead Merck Consumer Care*

"If you want a complete system to clarify your purpose, build your self-confidence and catapult your career success, you need this book! Just follow the step-by-step rules for guaranteeing your corporate career success."
  – *John Arigoni, President and CEO Boys and Girls Clubs of Metro Denver*

"Bud knows that everything counts when it comes to creating your corporate career success. Read and study this book if you want to climb the corporate ladder. Bud's easy going style makes learning and applying his keys to success an enjoyable and rewarding experience."
   – *Gary Ryan Blair, The Goals Guy, Bestselling Author of Everything Counts*

"Bud is a clever writer who tells fascinating stories that illuminate the points he makes. He covers practically any facet of corporate career success: from the basics; like grooming and thank you notes to personal character traits – confidence building, serving others and so much more. Bud is generous with his advice, sensitive to the reader's time and highly entertaining. This is a must read."
   – *Van Horsley, Senior Vice President Colorado Operations, First Citizens Bank & Trust Company*

Praise for Bud Bilanich's Previous Books

Straight Talk For Success

*"Straight Talk for Success…*As I read one common sense point after another, I was cheering the Common Sense Guy. I can't think of one person who wouldn't recognize themselves more than once in this book. We all need some Straight Talk. No matter how successful you are and how much common sense you think you have, you must read this book. Guarantee – you'll want everyone around you to read it too."
— *Diane Craig, President, Corporate Class Inc.*

"Bud 'The Common Sense Guy' Bilanich, has done it again... put together a roadmap for both career and life success. *Straight Talk for Success* is jam packed with hundreds of tactical and practical tools that leaders, at EVERY level, can apply immediately. Bottom line: this is one of the very best 'how to' success books I've ever read and I recommend it highly."
— *Eric Harvey, co-author, "Walk the Talk: And Get the Results You Want"*

"If you're interested in building a successful and fulfilling career, Bud Bilanich's book is a must-read! Bud understands what it takes to be successful and he distills his wisdom into an easily readable, fast paced text."
— *William Arruda, author of the bestselling careers book, "Career Distinction"*

"This fast-moving book is loaded with practical ideas and strategies you can apply immediately to achieve greater success."
— *Brian Tracy, author, "The Way to Wealth"*

4 Secrets of High Performing Organizations

"Elegantly simple."
  – *Karen Katen, President, Pfizer Global Pharmaceuticals*
    Executive Vice President, Pfizer, Inc

"Simple but powerful concepts."
  – *Chase Carey, CEO, Fox Television*

"Full of wisdom that applies to leaders of all types of organizations."
  – *John Arigoni, President and CEO, Boys and Girls Clubs of*
    Metro Denver

"Any leader, from CEO to mail room supervisor, will find easy-to-use ideas in this book."
  – *Ron Guziak, Executive Director, Hoag Hospital Foundation*

Using Values to Turn Vision into Reality

"A simple but powerful book. Read it!"
  – *Ken Blanchard*

"Refreshing and useful. Effectively takes important leadership concepts and brings them to life."
  – *Peggy Williams, President, Ithaca College*

"An excellent 'how-to' book on turning vision and values into value-added results."
  – *Eric Harvey, Co-author "Walk the Talk…and Get the*
    Results You Want"

Supervisory Leadership and the New Factory

"This book is must reading for anyone interested in managing an effective manufacturing organization."
   – *Tony Maddaluna, Vice President Manufacturing, Europe Pfizer, Inc*

Fixing Performance Problems

"This is a book I wish I had when I was beginning my career as an HR generalist."
   – *Sylvia Montero, Senior Vice President Human Resources, Pfizer, Inc*

"Dr. Bilanich has once again provided his readers with an easy to read, practical guide for managing performance. His new book provides simple, common sense ideas on fixing performance problems. This information is particularly useful in manufacturing environments. It provides an excellent guideline for middle managers and supervisors to use when dealing with difficult performance issues."
   – *J. R. Mulkey, Director of Operations, Adams and Brookhaven Plants, Minerals Technologies, Inc.*

"As entrepreneurs, we know firsthand the importance of fixing performance problems. Bud Bilanich's book is full of common sense advice on this subject. Anyone who owns a small business should read and study it."
   – *Jack Davis, Rob Likoff, Founders, Group DCA*

Large quantity orders are available from Front Row Press.

191 University Blvd., #414 • Denver, CO 80246 • 303.393.0446

Dedication

As always, this book is for Cathy, my everything.

Climbing
The Corporate
Ladder

Bud Bilanich
The Common Sense Guy

Contents

Prologue

In September 2011 I opened a membership site called My Corporate Climb. It's an internet based learning tool aimed at helping people create successful careers inside corporations. My members tell me that the material in My Corporate Climb is very helpful to them in climbing the corporate ladder.

Many of my members have asked me to consolidate my thoughts on corporate career success in one place. I've done that in this book. The ideas in *Climbing the Corporate Ladder* are a result of my 35+ years experience working for, and consulting to, many of the best known companies in the world.

This book contains my best, most up-to-date thoughts on creating your success inside a corporation. It is a great companion piece and reference guide to the career success advice inside My Corporate Climb.

If you're a member of My Corporate Climb, thank you. Use this book as a handy reference to the ideas on corporate career success I share every month.

If you're not a member, this book will introduce you to my thinking on corporate career success. You can use it as a standalone, but I think you'll find that it compliments membership in My Corporate Climb quite well.

You can watch a free webinar I did about My Corporate Climb by going to http://www.BudBilanich.com/mccwebinar. I urge you to spend an hour watching the webinar to see if membership in My

Corporate Climb can help you create the corporate career success you deserve.

Regardless please know that I am here for you. As the title of one of my other books says, I want you to succeed in your corporate climb. You can have a successful and rewarding career in the corporate world. Let me show you how.

Bud Bilanich

The Common Sense Guy

Denver, CO

March 2012

Introduction

In early 2011, I was reading an article about Robert Redford in the AARP Magazine – unfortunately, I'm old enough to be a member. The famous actor said, "When I got into this business, I had this naïve idea that I would let my work speak for me." That made me sit up and take notice because I'd heard something similar just the week before.

I had been invited to talk to the Women's Mentoring Group at a large corporate client. As I was speaking with the coordinator, she pulled out a list of things that are often career success-blockers for women. One of them was "thinking that your work will speak for itself."

For years, I have been telling my career success clients that when it comes to creating your life and career success, there is one myth that can get in your way. That myth is, "good performance is enough" or "your work will speak for itself."

Yes, you have to be a good performer to create your life and career success. But good performance alone won't result in creating the life and career success you want and deserve. I learned this the hard way. In a competitive world, good performance is just the price of admission to the career success sweepstakes.

In the following pages, I share a formula for corporate career success that I've developed in 15 years of work for large corporations and more than 20 years' experience consulting to them.

My Story ...

I was born into a working class family. My maternal grandparents emigrated from Poland. My grandfather worked in a factory in the town near Pittsburgh where I grew up. My father's parents were born in the United States but never went to school. My grandmother helped her mother run a boarding house for miners and then began working as a domestic when she was 10. When he was eight, my grandfather went to work in the coal mines.

My hometown was a company town called Ambridge. It was so named because the American Bridge Division of U.S. Steel was headquartered there. My father was an hourly worker for American Bridge for almost 40 years. My mother worked the checkout counter at a supermarket and then became an office manager at a Kmart.

Neither of my parents got anywhere near a college. Education, however, was big in our house. All I heard growing up was "go to college, go to college." In high school, I worked hard and got good grades and graduated from Penn State in 1972. I was a VISTA (Volunteers In Service To America) volunteer for a year and then began my career as a trainer – training other VISTA volunteers.

I didn't want to spend my life in government, so I went to night school to get a master's degree in two years, working 5:30 to 10:30 four nights a week. I worked full time and went to school full time and graduated with a 4.0 grade point average.

My first job in business was in the training department of a large oil company. I worked hard, did a good job – and kept getting passed over for promotion. The reasons were vague: "you've only been here a little while," "the hiring manager thought the other person was a better fit," "you need to polish some of those rough edges."

So I found another job, this time with a chemical company. I worked hard, did a good job, got good performance reviews – and still no promotions. I was frustrated. I knew I was as good as, or better than, the people who were moving ahead while I was standing still.

I decided that more schooling was the answer. I quit my job and enrolled in a PhD program in Adult Education and Organizational Behavior at Harvard University. This is when I realized that there was little difference between academia and business: The hardest workers and best performers weren't always rewarded and promoted.

I decided to use my situation as a lab. At Harvard, I was surrounded by high performers – those who had achieved a lot at an early age and seemed destined to achieve even more. I decided that I should pay attention to these folks.

Using one of those marble-covered notebooks, I listed those I admired at Harvard, those in the companies where I had worked who got promoted and those I considered role models. I began reading biographies of successful people. The list included Benjamin Franklin, George Washington, Thomas Jefferson, Winston Churchill, Ghandi, Malcolm X, Martin Luther King, Nelson Mandela. I created a page for each person. I wrote down their characteristics. When I finished, I had a notebook full of the characteristics of successful people.

It was a long list. So I did kind of a human regression analysis, looking for patterns and groups of behaviors. As a result, I concluded that successful people shared certain characteristics…

- They had a clearly defined purpose and direction for their lives.
- They were committed to succeeding and overcame obstacles.
- They were self-confident, knowing they would succeed and continue to succeed.
- They were outstanding performers.
- They presented themselves favorably and attracted others to them.
- They were dynamic communicators.
- They were good at relationship building.

Once I finished my degree, I went to work for a pharmaceutical company in New York. I applied the lessons learned from observing successful people – and I began getting good assignments and promotions. I became the confidant of senior executives, and I began coaching "up-and-comers" in the company – teaching them the principles I had discovered from my observations in that marble-covered notebook.

I also kept refining my ideas, making them easier for others to understand and apply. You never learn something as thoroughly as when you teach it. I became the company's most sought-after internal coach.

In 1988, I was faced with a decision: Accept promotion to Vice President or strike out on my own. I have an entrepreneurial bent and chose the latter. I started a consulting, coaching and speaking business. The idea was to reach even greater numbers of people with what I knew about creating a successful life and career.

For many years, I thrived as a corporate consultant. Then I got cancer – and survived. I realized that there was more to life than working as a highly paid consultant. I had an opportunity to reach even more people with my common sense message, people I would never get a chance to meet working one-on-one with executives in large companies.

That's why I'm making everything I know about life and career success available. It's why I wrote this book. I want to help as many people as I can create the successful lives and careers they deserve. I survived a cancer scare and now I want to give as much as I can to as many people as I can.

My Corporate Climb is based on seven simple, but powerful, common sense ideas:

1. Clarity of purpose and direction
2. Commitment to taking personal responsibility for your life and career
3. Unshakable self-confidence
4. Outstanding performance
5. Positive personal impact
6. Dynamic communication
7. Relationship building

The seven principles have guided me on my success journey. I'm sharing them so they can guide you on your personal journey to career and life success. Let's look at them in more detail.

The keys to developing your clarity of purpose and direction are…

- Defining what success means to you personally.
- Creating a vivid mental picture of yourself as a success.
- Clarifying your personal values.

The keys to committing to your success are…

- Taking personal responsibility for your success.
- Setting high goals and doing what it takes to achieve them.
- Choosing to respond positively to people and events.

The keys to becoming self-confident are…

- Choosing optimism, believing that today will be better than yesterday and tomorrow will be better than today.
- Facing your fears and acting, refusing to let your fears paralyze you into inaction.
- Surrounding yourself with positive people and jettisoning nay-sayers in your life.

There are four keys to becoming an outstanding performer. You have to…

- Update your skills by becoming a lifelong learner.
- Understand that business runs on numbers. Know your company and industry's finances.
- Manage your time, life and stress.
- Live a healthy lifestyle.

The four keys to creating positive personal impact are...

- Develop strength of character.
- Create and nurture your unique personal brand.
- Be impeccable in your presentation of self, in person and online.
- Follow the rules of business etiquette.

The keys to becoming a dynamic communicator are...

- Communicate well in conversation.
- Communicate well in writing.
- Communicate well in presentations.

The keys to building strong relationships are...

- Understanding yourself so that self-understanding helps you understand others. Paying it forward and without expecting a return.
- Resolving conflict in a way that strengthens, not destroys, the relationships you've built.

I know this sounds like a tall order when you see and hear it like this. The ideas can seem a bit overwhelming. That's why I've written this book – to help you take it slowly, one step at a time. The ideas in the book build on one another. By the time you've finished the book, you'll know what you need to do to succeed – you'll be on your way to unstoppable success.

Section 1

Clarity of Purpose and Direction

George Bernard Shaw, the Irish playwright, is one of my favorite writers. I always enjoy productions of his plays. He was a hard worker – someone who was committed to his craft. He makes a great point about how important personal clarity of purpose and direction is to career and life success.

"This is the true joy in life; being used for a purpose recognized by yourself as a mighty one; being a force of nature instead of a feverish, selfish little clod of ailments and grievances complaining that the world will not devote itself to making you happy."

He's talking about two things here: accomplishing a lot – being a "force of nature" – and more important, having a mighty purpose to direct that force. Clarity of purpose and direction is one of the seven keys to your corporate career success. You can develop it by doing three things. First, define what success means to you personally. Second, create a vivid mental image of yourself as a success. This image should be as vivid as you can make it. Third, clarify your personal values.

Your clarity of purpose and direction is your foundation to build the successful life and career that you want. The clearer and more mighty your purpose and direction, the stronger your foundation will be.

I'm a 1960s guy. After all these years, my favorite recording artist is still Bob Dylan. My favorite Dylan song – and maybe my favorite song ever – is "Forever Young." He re-recorded and re-released it not long ago. Pepsi picked it up and used it in ads that ran during professional football games. I used a line from the song to introduce my bestselling book *Straight Talk for Success* – "May you build a ladder to the stars and climb on every rung."

Check out some of the other lyrics…

> "May your hands always be busy
> May your feet always be swift
> May you have a strong foundation
> When the winds of changes shift."

By now, you may be saying, "Let's get to the point, Bud." So I will. You need to begin your corporate success journey by clarifying your purpose in life. Why are you on Earth? What were you meant to do? I believe that the more mighty the purpose, the more likely you will succeed. A mighty purpose provides the foundation for "when the winds of changes shift."

As a career success coach, I help others succeed in realizing their purpose. I believe this is a mighty purpose. I may help someone who could become president or a member of the Supreme Court or someone who finds a cure for cancer or just a loving and caring parent. This purpose anchors me. It keeps me going when I'm frustrated or when I feel like quitting. Or when I start to feel that it's OK to be "good enough," instead of great.

The other day, I was having a conversation with one of my career success clients. We were talking about the *My Corporate Climb* model. More specifically, we were discussing clarity of purpose and direction. She told me that she had read a blog post on clarity of purpose and direction I had written. She added that she was confused by all the different words that came up when she thought about clarity – words like purpose, direction, mission and vision.

This got me to thinking: If she gets confused about the semantics of clarity of purpose and direction, I bet others do, too. This is why I defined these terms in a way that will help you create your personal clarity of purpose and direction.

Note that these are the working definitions I use in my model of corporate career success. You may have seen other definitions for these terms. I am presenting them here to help you better understand how I use them in my model – not as the "correct" definition of these terms.

For our purposes, I define the word "mission" as …

- Your **reason** for existing.
- Your **passion**.
- **Why** you are on Earth.

This isn't always easy to discover.

If you're young and still trying to figure out your mission, don't worry. It takes time. That's why I always tell people to be open to new ideas and thoughts. After all, you never know what you might pick up.

Had you told me in high school that my mission would be helping others succeed, I would have laughed. It took several courses in college and a year as a VISTA volunteer for me to figure it out. That's when I began my career in the human development field.

Your mission needs to come from deep inside. It is unlikely to change over the long run. I've had lots of jobs in lots of companies and have been self-employed for almost 25 years. Through all the changes, one thing remains constant – my desire and passion for helping others succeed. In my heart of hearts, I know that I am on Earth to help others navigate the ambiguities of life in order to reach their goals.

Here is my mission…

> To help others achieve the career and life success that they want and deserve by applying their common sense.

It hasn't changed since I was 23. This mission reflects who I am and why I get up each morning. It's what's right for me.

What's right for you? What is your passion? What is your reason for living? Why are you on Earth?

Think of your vision as…

- Where you are going
- What you will achieve in the next 1, 5, 10 and 20 years.

Unlike your mission, your vision will likely change over your life and career. Early in my career, I worked for the government, training VISTA volunteers. My three-year vision was to earn a master's degree at night and to parlay that into a training and development job in business. You'll note that this vision fit into my mission of helping others succeed in their lives and careers but had a specific short-term time frame.

When I was in my 30s, my vision shifted. It became "to create a successful, one-person coaching, consulting and speaking business." Your vision needs to be consistent with your mission. Unlike your mission, however, your vision should change as you grow and develop in your career.

Finally, your vision should always be a BHAG – a big hairy audacious goal. I first saw this term in Jim Collins and Jerry Porras' great book *Built to Last*. You need to create a vision that will challenge and motivate you – it should be big and hairy and audacious. What's a big hairy audacious goal for the next year? Five years? Ten years?

My current vision comes in a one-year and a five-year time frame:

- Create a profitable Internet business that will allow me to share my optimistic message on life and career success and help as many people as I can.
- Make 100% of my income from the Internet five years from now.

Notice how my one-year vision is consistent with my mission of helping others succeed in their lives and careers. It's also a BHAG – for me at least. I've accumulated knowledge about career and life success over a lifetime of work and study. But turning that knowledge into information products I can sell on the Internet is something new for me. I'm learning about Internet marketing as I go. With a little luck and a lot of persistence, I'm confident that this will be my breakout year as an Internet marketer.

I'm also confident that in five years I'll be doing almost all my business on the Internet. I'll be traveling for business only when I choose to. This will be a radical departure from the 45 weeks of business travel that I've logged for many years.

So, where does all this leave us when it comes to thinking about clarity of purpose and direction? Here's how I suggest you think about it.

Your purpose is your mission – your reason for living, your passion, what you are here to do, something unlikely to change over the long run.

Your direction is your vision – short- and medium-term goals that define the direction you will take your life and career.

There is a common sense point here. Successful people define clarity of purpose and direction for their lives and careers. Your clarity of purpose and direction should include both a personal mission (your purpose) and a personal vision (your direction). Your mission is your reason for living, why you are here on Earth. It is unlikely to change over the long run. Your vision is a short- or medium-term goal that defines the direction you'll take over the next three to five years. This will change as you grow and develop in your life and career. Your vision must be consistent with your mission.

Brad Swift of the Life On Purpose Institute (www.lifeonpurpose. com) makes a great point about clarity of purpose…

"Taking a bold stand for living on purpose starts by knowing your purpose with crystal clarity – knowing it so well that if someone woke you up at 3:00 in the morning and asked you what your life purpose is, you'd be able to tell them. And if someone who knew you well heard what you said, they'd realize that your life was a true, authentic reflection of that purpose."

There are two common sense points I want to focus on here. First, clarity of purpose has to be deeply ingrained in your psyche. It has to be part of who you are. Second, you have to live your clarity of purpose 24/7/365. This takes commitment: commitment to determining your life's purpose and commitment to living it.

Several years ago, I decided that my life's purpose was to help others create successful lives and careers. I take great satisfaction in seeing others learn, grow and succeed. In another life, I might have been a teacher or athletic coach. In this life, I help people succeed in business.

If you were to wake me at 3:00 in the morning, shine a light in my face and ask me for my life's purpose, I would say, "Helping people create the life and career success they want and deserve." It's that much a part of me. My elevator speech begins, "Hi, I'm Bud Bilanich, the Common Sense Guy. I help people create successful lives and careers by applying their common sense."

What is your purpose in life? Is it deeply ingrained in you? Have you even thought about it?

Clarity of purpose and direction comes first in my corporate career success model. As I mentioned, my purpose is to help other people create successful lives and careers by applying their common sense. That has been a constant with me through my entire working life. My direction has changed over the years. Recently, it has changed dramatically. My vision for the next five years is to build an Internet-based coaching and career development business. That's where I'm going. It's why I write a blog and publish an ezine. It's why I've begun sending my subscribers daily "Think, Act, Succeed" quotes. It's why I wrote this book.

Your direction defines what you do every day. It should reinforce your life purpose. Clarifying not only your purpose but your direction helps get you to the second of Brad Swift's points: "If someone who knew you well heard what you said (about your life's purpose), they'd realize that your life was a true and authentic reflection of that purpose." That's why I believe that clarity of purpose and clarity of direction are equally important.

Clarity of direction helps you determine what you are going to do every minute and every hour of every day. If your direction is congruent with your purpose, others will notice. More important, you'll be living your purpose and creating the successful life and career you deserve.

Successful people clarify their purpose and direction in life. They understand what success means to them and have a vivid mental image of themselves as a success. Everything they do is consistent with their clarity of purpose. Their day-to-day actions move them closer to their vision of success and are consistent with their clarity of purpose. When you clarify your purpose, and live it, you will hardly ever procrastinate or find yourself going off on a tangent. You'll be laser-focused on living the life that's important to you. What's your clarity of purpose? Are you living it?

Dr. Martin Luther King is one of my heroes. I contributed to the fund for his monument on the Mall in Washington, D.C. that was dedicated in August 2011. Dr. King helped lead our nation out of the dehumanizing segregation that existed in for generations. More than any other person, I believe he was responsible for passage of the Civil Rights Act of 1964. Today, a black man is president of the United States. This would have been unthinkable back in 1963 when Dr. King delivered his famous "I Have a Dream" speech.

I bring up Dr. King's speech because it is the embodiment of clarity of purpose and direction. Read the words and see how they clearly describe his vision of success, for himself and the nation, and how they vividly depict what success meant to him.

"And so even though we face the difficulties of today and tomorrow, I still have a dream. It is a dream deeply rooted in the American dream.

I have a dream that one day this nation will rise up and live out the true meaning of its creed: 'We hold these truths to be self-evident, that all men are created equal.'

I have a dream that one day on the red hills of Georgia, the sons of former slaves and the sons of former slave owners will be able to sit down together at the table of brotherhood.

I have a dream that one day even the state of Mississippi, a state sweltering with the heat of injustice, sweltering with the heat of oppression, will be transformed into an oasis of freedom and justice.

I have a dream that my four little children will one day live in a nation where they will not be judged by the color of their skin but by the content of their character.

I have a *dream* today!

I have a dream that one day, *down* in Alabama, with its

vicious racists, with its governor having his lips dripping with the words of 'interposition' and 'nullification' – one day right there in Alabama, little black boys and black girls will be able to join hands with little white boys and white girls as sisters and brothers.

I have a *dream* today!

I have a dream that one day every valley shall be exalted, and every hill and mountain shall be made low, the rough places will be made plain, and the crooked places will be made straight; and the glory of the Lord shall be revealed and all flesh shall see it together."

Those are powerful words. Can you see how they demonstrate Dr. King's clarity of purpose and direction? He carried on his work well after the Civil Rights Act of 1964 became law because he knew that legislation alone does not bring about change in society.

What is your dream? Can you articulate it as clearly and vividly as Dr. King?

Dr. King also lived his personal values. One of his quotes is sadly prophetic: "A man who won't die for something is not fit to live."

Dr. King was gunned down on April 4, 1968, in Memphis by James Earl Ray. His legacy and message are still celebrated today – more than 40 years after his death.

There is a common sense point in this discussion of Dr. King's "I Have a Dream" speech. Few people have demonstrated such a clear sense of purpose and direction for their lives as Dr. Martin

Luther King. His speech is one of the best examples of a vivid description of not only personal success, but success for us as a society. "I have a dream…that little black boys and black girls will be able to join hands with little white boys and white girls as sisters and brothers." The dream is alive – although we still need to keep working on it.

Chapter 1

Develop Your Personal Definition of Career Success

I n my book *4 Secrets of High Performing Organizations,* I point out that all successful, high-performing organizations have four things in common: clarity of purpose and direction; the sincere commitment of all the organization's members; skillful execution of the things that matter; and mutually beneficial relationships with important outside constituencies.

Clarity of purpose and direction is also fundamental to your corporate career success. It all begins with a clear picture of how you define career success.

If you'd asked me when I was 25 what I wanted to be doing when I was 50, I would have said, "Running a one-person coaching, consulting and speaking business from my home." Guess what? I have been running a one-person consulting, coaching and speaking business since 1988. Clarity of purpose propelled me toward my goal.

I have a friend who is a serial entrepreneur. At 27, he started a software business. By the time he was 35, he had built it up and sold it to a major computer manufacturer. He has since started and sold four other companies. His clarity of purpose lies in the challenge of creating something new, building it into a viable, sustainable business and then moving on.

I have another friend who recently retired as the Executive VP of Human Resources for a Fortune 50 company. We were chatting a few days ago. She told me that when she was in college, she decided that she was going to join a good company and work her way up the ladder. She took an entry-level HR job with a company she liked. It took her more than 25 years but she became the senior HR executive in the company. Her clarity of purpose and definition of success was different from mine and the serial entrepreneur's but she reached her goal.

My friend told me that her son has a different definition of success. He isn't interested in climbing the corporate ladder or in being an entrepreneur. He wants an interesting job where he can contribute but doesn't want to spend inordinate time at work. He wants to spend as much time with his family as he can. His definition of corporate career success is different from his mother's.

All four of us are career successes – according to our clarity of purpose.

There is no one correct definition of career success. There are as many definitions as there are people in this world. Your definition of career success is what's right for you – not someone else. I would not have been happy building and selling a number of businesses in succession, climbing the corporate ladder or working for a large company in an individual contributor position. As you can tell from the stories of the three people here, they were. They knew what they wanted and they went after it.

That's why defining your clarity of purpose is so important. Your clarity of purpose is a foundation and a launching pad for your career success. The saying, "If you don't know where you're going, you won't know when you get there" is a cliché. But like all cliché's, it's true. Getting clear on your personal definition of career success is your first step to becoming a career success.

If you haven't already done it, take time to think about your clarity of purpose. How do you define career success for yourself? Keep that purpose and definition of success in mind as you read this book. Think about how the information that follows can help you reach your purpose.

Chapter 2

Create a Vivid Mental Image of Yourself as a Success

B egin creating your vivid mental image of yourself as a career success with affirmations. Affirmations are positive self-talk. The idea behind them is simple. When you think of the things you aspire to, like becoming a career success, tell yourself that you are a career success, and you'll believe that you can become one. More important, you'll be more likely to do the work it takes to make that aspiration come true.

For example, if you're in a new job, say to yourself, "I have the skills and desire to succeed in this job," several times a day. If you repeat this often enough, you'll begin to believe it. This will help you perform at the level needed to succeed in your job.

A couple of years ago, I wrote a book *Star Power, Common*

Sense Ideas for Career and Life Success. I used a star to depict the ideas in the book. I urged readers to think of themselves as a star and to aspire to becoming a life and career star. I like the star metaphor. Each day, I repeat this affirmation: "Bud Bilanich is a star."

I've done a lot of work to make the affirmation a reality – re-doing my website, developing better promotional materials, speaking, writing books and blogging.

I've also done something a little unusual. A few years ago, right after *Star Power* was published, I went to the "Name a Star" website and named a star after myself. Now, I can say "Bud Bilanich is a star" and really believe it because Bud Bilanich really is a star. It's easy for me to visualize myself as a star because I am a star.

Bud Bilanich, the star, is Catalog Number TYC 868-1011-1 in the constellation Leo. Bud Bilanich has a Visual Magnitude indicator of 11.2. Right Ascension is 11h 58m 21s. Declination is 11 degrees, 43'18." I don't have a clue what these things mean except that they refer to the constellation Leo, which I chose because my birthday is August 14. But I do know one thing: Bud Bilanich is a star!

How's that for an affirmation?

Affirmations work. I have become a minor star in the life and career success coaching world. You don't need to go to the lengths I did to make affirmations work. Just decide what you want, visualize yourself as having it and tell yourself you have it. Then do whatever it takes to make the affirmation come true.

Affirmations alone, however, are not enough to guarantee career success. You have to do the work. Spend the time needed to accomplish your goals. Volunteer for projects that will get you noticed. Become an expert on your company, its competitors and your industry. In other words, bust your butt and you'll succeed.

To develop a vivid mental image of your career success, you need to think through your priorities – and then align your behavior to be sure you live according to them. Ask yourself two questions:

1. What do I want to do in my life and career?
2. What is the result I want to achieve?

The answers will not only guide the big decisions you make, they'll be a guide for living your life on a day-to-day basis.

Here's another way to look at it. Imagine that you're nearing the end of your life. You feel happy, content and satisfied. You don't fear death because you've had a happy and prosperous life and career. You've lived and loved, succeeded in your chosen field and feel you've been blessed.

Once you get yourself into this frame of mind, look back at your life and career and what you've accomplished. Of all your accomplishments, what matters the most to you? What challenges did you overcome to realize these accomplishments? How did you do it? What messages did you send to others by the way you lived your life and career?

This visualization exercise can help you create a vivid mental image of your life and career success. This is an important exercise because it will help make clear what career success looks like for you personally. This is not daydreaming. It's real work. You are designing your future career success in your mind.

After a lot of thinking and reflection, I realized that my purpose in life is simple – to help others grow and succeed. I am a teacher and a helper. I enjoy helping others succeed. I'm good at it. It's fulfilling. At the end of my life, I expect to look back with satisfaction at the number of people I helped to create successful lives and careers.

I keep this mental picture as I go about my day-to-day business. I ask a simple question every day: "Bud, did the things you did today support your life's purpose of helping others learn, grow and succeed?"

If the answer is "yes," I consider it a successful day. If the answer is "no," I think about what I can do the next day to get back to living my purpose. I have a clear and vivid mental image of what success means to me. It helps me live my life's purpose every day. If you haven't clarified your purpose in life, this is a good time to start. Once you get clear on your purpose, live it every day in all your actions.

Once you define what success means to you, I suggest that you develop a clear mental picture of your career success. This image should be as vivid as you can make it.

When I was 25, I conjured up an image of myself as a successful career coach, motivational speaker, management consultant and author. I worked in my home office, where I wrote and developed the programs I delivered at client locations. This office had a floor-to-ceiling wall of books that I could use for easy reference. It also had a state-of-the-art IBM Selectric typewriter and a big, clunky telephone. In 1975, PCs and the Internet belonged to science fiction.

I also saw myself having one-to-one discussions with senior

leaders in a variety of organizations, conducting training and team-building sessions in their conference rooms. Amazingly, many of the people in the sessions were smoking. I had very vivid images of standing in front of large audiences at sales meetings. I saw myself in a book store signing a book I had written. I also saw myself on airplanes traveling to my speaking, coaching and consulting gigs.

All of these images came true. My office is much as I had imagined it – except that it has two PCs and a cell phone, not an electric typewriter and a clunky phone. The wall of books is there – overflowing. I've written 14 of the books. People don't smoke in my training and team-building sessions anymore. Instead of handwritten flip charts, I use PowerPoint but the big stuff is the same as I always imagined it. I've spoken to audiences in Latin America, Europe, Asia and all over North America. I am a million-mile flyer with Continental Air Lines.

I'm living my career success dream in large part because I dared to dream it years ago.

What's your career success dream? Have you created a vivid mental image of it?

I suggest that you take some time for yourself. Ask and answer these questions:

- Where do I want to be 10, 20 and 30 years from now?
- What will it look like and feel like when I'm there?
- What will my life be like?

Ask and answer any other questions that will help you develop a clear and vivid mental image of your career success. By doing this, you'll be designing your future career success in your own mind.

Keep this mental picture with you as you go about your day-to-day business. Every once in a while, ask yourself if what you did that day brought you closer to your mental image of success. This way, you'll be keeping your dream alive – and moving toward your goal.

The common sense point here is simple. Successful people define what success means to them. Then they develop a compelling and clear mental image of their success. They use this image to help keep their dreams alive and to move toward their life and career success. Creating a vivid mental image of your career success is the real work of designing your future so that you can take the steps to create it.

Chapter 3

Clarify Your Values

Y our personal values are a composite of your life experiences and major influences. These can include people like your parents and family, friends and peers, and things like your religion, education and reading habits.

Your values impact every aspect of your life. You demonstrate them in your personal and work behavior, decision-making and interactions with others. You use your values to make decisions in your work and home life. Your goals and life purpose are grounded in your values.

Regardless of your life experiences and influences, you can choose the values that are most important to you, things you believe in that define your character. Living in harmony with your values is the best way to become the person you want to be and to achieve life and career success.

Very simply, values are those things that are important to you. They are the embodiment of what you stand for as a human being.

Your personal values are your guide to decision-making in ambiguous situations. They guide your life. You make decisions based on your values every day. We all do.

One of my clients turned down a big promotion recently. When I asked why, he said, "The job I was offered would have meant relocating. My family is very important to me. I have two kids in high school. I wasn't willing to disrupt their lives at this point. I'm sure other opportunities will come along in three years when both of them are out of the house and in college."

This client was staying true to his value of family. He was willing to put his career success on hold for a few years to provide a stable home life and high school experience for his kids. He told me that he didn't have to think hard about turning down the promotional opportunity. His family value was that deeply ingrained in him.

Let's take another example. Many people value their personal integrity. One way they demonstrate this value is telling a cashier that he or she has given them change for $20 bill when in fact they paid with a ten.

These examples are clear cut. Your personal values, however, are most valuable when you face an ambiguous situation. They will guide you and help you make the best possible decision.

When you are job hunting, find a company that has values similar to yours. You'll fit in better and be more comfortable if you do. During the job interview, ask questions like: "What's it like to work here?" "How important is integrity at this company?" "What do you like most about working here?" "What do you like least about working here?"

If you read between the lines, you'll get a good idea about the values of the company. This will help you decide if you want to work for them. A good fit between personal values and company values will make your work life more pleasant and fulfilling and will put you on the road to the career success you deserve.

Section 2

Commit to Your Career Success

C ommitment to taking personal responsibility for your career success is one of the seven keys to career success. If you want to succeed, you must commit to three things. First, take personal responsibility for your career success. Only you can make you a career success. You need to be willing to do the things necessary to succeed. Second, set high goals – and then do whatever it takes to achieve them. Third, stuff happens: As you go through life, you will encounter many problems and setbacks. You need to react positively to the negative stuff and move forward toward your goals.

I live in Denver, where the weather is very changeable. On December 21, 2009, the first day of winter, we had 60-degree weather. That night, the weather announcer on TV reminded us that we had snow on the last day of summer.

This got me to thinking about the unpredictability of life. As I often say, stuff happens in life – good stuff, bad stuff, happy stuff, sad stuff, encouraging stuff and frustrating stuff. It isn't the fact that stuff happens that matters, it's how you react to it. You can't control the people and events in your life. You can control how you react to them.

I choose to react positively to the people and events in my life – especially the bad, sad and frustrating stuff. And I urge you to do the same, if you want to create the life and career success you deserve.

I know it isn't always easy. In fact, it's seldom easy. But the harder you find it to react positively to negative people and events, the more important it is for you to do it. When things go wrong, don't blame people or circumstances. Instead, try to learn the lesson behind every unsuccessful relationship or event.

When you look for the lessons behind problems, setbacks and failures, you're taking responsibility for your life and career success. Find the lessons in the bad stuff and then do something to put the lessons to work. When it came to figuring out how to make a light bulb, Edison said he never failed—he just found 10,000 ways that didn't work.

Take up Edison's spirit. Commit to taking responsibility for yourself, your life and your career success. Put yourself in the driver's seat. Don't let events and people stop you from achieving your goals and career success. Be persistent.

As I write this, I'm reminded of a famous quote of Calvin Coolidge…

> "Nothing in the world can take the place of persistence. Talent will not; nothing is more common than unsuccessful men with talent. Genius will not; unrewarded genius is almost a proverb. Education will not; the world is full of educated failures. Persistence and determination alone are omnipotent."

The common sense point here is simple. Successful people commit to taking personal responsibility for their life and career and career success. Only you can make you a success. You have to take personal responsibility for creating the successful life and career you want and deserve. Persistence is the mark of those committed to taking responsibility for their lives and careers. Persistent people keep going, even in – no, especially in – the face of difficulties and problems. Promise yourself that you will commit to taking personal responsibility for your life and career in 2010. Be persistent. Keep at it and you'll reach your goals.

The other day, I saw a great quote from Margaret Thatcher...

> "Look at a day when you are supremely satisfied at the end. It's not a day when you lounge around doing nothing; it's when you've had everything to do, and you've done it."

The Iron Lady really nailed it with that one! I like this quote because it gets to the essence of the commitment to take personal responsibility for your life and career. Commitment to personal responsibility is one of the seven keys to success I discuss in this book. I discuss it in several of my other books: *Straight Talk for Success; Star Power; I want YOU...To Succeed; Your Success GPS;* and *42 Rules to Jumpstart Your Professional Success.*

As I've said, you demonstrate your commitment to your career success – to yourself and to the world – by doing three things. First, take personal responsibility for your success. Second, set high goals – and then do whatever it takes to achieve them. Third, recognize that stuff happens and react positively to problems and setbacks so that you can move forward toward your goals.

Those days where you have a lot to do and get it done are not only satisfying, they demonstrate your commitment to success and help strengthen it. I'm writing this on a plane at 8:00 on a Friday night. I've been up since 5:00 a.m. because I had to finish an important project for a client before an all-day workshop with Russell Brunson, my Internet marketing mentor and business partner. I've had a full day, and Mrs. Thatcher would agree it's one in which I feel a sense of supreme satisfaction. I've demonstrated to myself that I'm willing to do the things necessary to succeed.

On the other hand, I had a bout with the flu this past winter. It left me feeling weak and tired. I spent all of a Monday afternoon and a good part of a Tuesday morning in bed. It couldn't be helped. I needed to get my strength back. By Tuesday afternoon, I was feeling better physically but I was emotionally drained. I felt as if I hadn't moved forward toward my career success goals. I didn't get anything done for about 24 hours – and I hated it.

I agree not only with Margaret Thatcher, but with George Bernard Shaw, who said…

> "I am of the opinion that my life belongs to the whole community, and as long as I live it is my privilege to do for it whatever I can. I want to be thoroughly used up when I die, for the harder I work, the more I live. I rejoice in life for its own sake. Life is no 'brief candle' for me. It is a sort of splendid torch which I have got hold of for the moment, and I want to make it burn as brightly as possible before handing it on to future generations."

I know that I want my life to be a splendid torch that burns long and brightly. How about you? Do you revel in hard work and accomplishing everything you can? Or do you prefer those days Mrs. Thatcher described as one where you "lounge around doing nothing?"

Successful people relish the days when they have a lot to do, and then go on and do it. They get satisfaction from working hard and seeing the results of their labor. When was the last day you were truly busy? How did you feel at the end of the day? If you're an achiever – someone committed to your career and life success – I bet you were exhilarated and ready to take on the next day.

I have a favorite Japanese proverb…

Vision without action is a daydream.
Action without vision is a nightmare.

This proverb is a twofer on clarity of purpose and direction and committing to your career success.

"Vision without action is a daydream" goes to the heart of commitment. No matter how big your plans, thoughts and dreams, they'll never become a reality until you act on them. You have to commit to taking personal responsibility for creating your successful life and career. And action is the single most important word when it comes to demonstrating commitment.

On the other hand, action without vision is a nightmare. You'll never get where you want to go if you don't have a clear idea of what you want to achieve. I call this clarity of purpose and direction. Think of your purpose as your mission in life: why you exist, why you are in the world. Think of your direction as your vision for the next five years, that big hairy audacious goal you're going to accomplish. Your mission and vision, your purpose and direction shape your actions. When you act in accordance with them, you'll avoid the nightmares that come from unfocused action.

The common sense point here is simple. Successful people have a clearly defined purpose and direction for their lives. They also commit to taking personal responsibility for their lives and careers. To develop your clarity of purpose and direction, you need to do three things. First, define what success means to you personally. Second, create a vivid mental image of yourself as a success. This should be as vivid as you can make it. Third, clarify your personal values. You demonstrate your commitment to taking personal responsibility for your life and career by doing three things. First, take personal responsibility for your success. Only you can make you a success. You must be willing to do the things necessary to succeed. Second, set high goals – and then do whatever it takes to achieve them. Third, recognize that stuff happens in life. React positively to problems and setbacks so that you can move forward toward your goals. Getting clear and getting committed are the starting points for creating your successful life and career.

Commitment to taking personal responsibility for your career and life success is what Bernard Shaw is talking about when he says we should be "a force of nature instead of a feverish, selfish little clod of ailments and grievances complaining that the world will not devote itself to making you happy." Man, that guy could write! "Selfish little clod of ailments and grievances" – that's really turning a phrase. What he means is that you need to take personal responsibility – commit to it. Yeah, stuff happens as you go through life. Some of it is frustrating and annoying. But successful people react to the frustrating stuff by choosing to react positively. They learn from difficult situations and people and then go on to bigger and better things. They aren't selfish little clods of ailments and grievances.

Chapter 4

Take Personal Responsibility for Your Success

I t's simple, really. Success is up to you and me and anyone else who wants it. We all have to take personal responsibility for our own success. I am the only one who can make me a success. You are the only one who can make you a success.

Stuff happens: good stuff, bad stuff, frustrating stuff, unexpected stuff. Successful people respond to the stuff of life in a positive way. Man is the only animal with free will. That means we – you and me – get to decide how we react to each situation. That's why taking personal responsibility for your career success is so important.

Personal responsibility means recognizing and accepting that you are responsible for your life and the choices you make. It means you realize that, while other people and events have an impact on your life, they don't shape your life. When you accept personal responsibility for your life, you own up to the fact that how you react to people and events is what's important. And you can choose how to react to everyone you meet and everything that happens to you.

The concept of personal responsibility can be found in most writing on success. Stephen Covey's first habit in *The 7 Habits of Highly Effective People* is "Be proactive." My friend John Miller's book *QBQ: the Question Behind the Question* asks readers to pose questions to themselves like, "What can I do to become a top performer?" John really believes that taking personal responsibility for your life and career is the key to your corporate career success.

The seven keys to success in this book work only if you are willing to take responsibility for your life and career. Personal responsibility is the foundation all life and career success is built on.

Personal responsibility means using the ideas in this book once you learn them. I've written it to provide you with useful information and knowledge on becoming a corporate career success. But as the U.S. Steel pencils that my father brought home from work used to say, "Knowing is not enough."

When I was a kid, I was really fascinated and puzzled by these pencils. "Knowing is not enough – what does that mean?" I spent hours struggling with the idea. I was too stubborn to ask a grown-up.

In my freshman year at Penn State, I took Philosophy 101. We had to read Johann von Goethe. As I was plowing through an assignment one day, I came across this quote: "Knowing is not enough, we must do. Willing is not enough, we must apply."

Was I glad I took that course! It solved one of the profound mysteries of my childhood: "Knowing is not enough." As I understand it, you have to take what you learn and use it, or what you've learned isn't very valuable. Part of personal responsibility is using your knowledge to achieve your goals.

This book will provide you with ideas on what to do to create your personal and corporate career success. It's up to you to think about these ideas, decide how you are going to use them and then put them to work. It's what personal responsibility is all about.

Chapter 5

Set High Goals – and Achieve Them

Set high goals for yourself – and then achieve them. Set S.M.A.R.T. (Specific, Measurable, Achievable, Results Oriented and Time Bound) goals. Come up with milestones for accomplishing your goals. Milestones are steps along the way to goal achievement. They keep you on track and motivate you by giving you reason to celebrate when you reach them.

All successful people set goals. Then they meet or exceed them. They do this day after day, week after week, month after month, year after year. I'm 61 and have been in business for myself for 23 years. I set goals every year and develop quarterly milestones for them. I measure myself against my goals and milestones. It's a habit I developed when I was first out of college. It's served me well over the years.

One of my favorite quotes on goal-setting is from Daniel Burnham: "Make no little plans. They have no magic to stir men's blood and probably will not be realized. Make big plans. Aim high in hope and work."

If you're going to set goals, you might as well set big ones. As Mr. Burnham says, big goals will "stir your blood." He ought to know, he designed landmarks that include the Flatiron Building in New York and Union Station in Washington, D.C.

I agree with Mr. Burnham: Many set their sights too low. They make little – instead of big – plans. I think people do this because they lack self-confidence. Self-confidence is an important key to success. Facing your fears and acting is one way to become self-confident. Making big plans and setting big goals are other ways of facing your fears and acting.

In *Built to Last,* Jim Collins and Jerry Porras suggest that successful companies need to set what they call "BHAGs" – Big Hairy Audacious Goals. Collins' follow up book *Good to Great* begins with the idea that "good is the enemy of great," an extension of the BHAG idea. The same kind of thinking holds for individuals. If you set big hairy audacious goals for yourself, you won't be settling for good, you'll be planning for great.

One of Henry David Thoreau's most repeated lines, "Most men lead lives of quiet desperation and go to the grave with the song still in them," applies here. Don't take your song to the grave. Sing it while you're alive. You can do this if you are willing to dare by setting high goals. And then doing whatever it takes to achieve them.

I have a framed piece of inspiration hanging in my office. It's this quote by Paul J. Meyer: "Whatever you vividly imagine, ardently desire, sincerely believe, and enthusiastically act upon... must inevitably come to pass!"

The key words here are "enthusiastically act upon." You have to do the work. I think this quote is the missing piece of advice in *The Secret*. In fact, I've often said that Paul Meyer's quote is like *The Secret* on steroids.

Successful people are outstanding performers. People become outstanding performers by setting and achieving high – no, big hairy audacious – goals. Outstanding performers put in the time and effort, the blood, sweat and tears necessary to turn their goals into reality. They don't settle for good because they know that good is the enemy of great. They choose to be great. They make no little plans. They make big plans that stir the blood.

Here are some easy steps to accomplish any goal…

Get focused. Make sure your goals are specific and measurable. The best goals are tightly focused. They are also measurable. For example, when I was writing this book, I set a goal of completing the first draft by June 30, 2011. As you can see, this goal is specific – finish a first draft of a book by a certain date. It is also measurable. I had a first draft completed by the date I set. Setting a date is a good way to measure your goal achievement. It is a very clear measure. You either accomplished your goal by that date or you didn't.

Ask why. Ask yourself, "Why do I want to accomplish this goal?" The answer will provide you with the focus and motivation you need to keep plugging away when you encounter setbacks. I wanted to write this book because it would help me communicate my thoughts on life and career success.

Get help. It's difficult to do everything by yourself. Identify friends and co-workers who can help you accomplish your goals. Most people are willing to help, if you ask them. I had several people read drafts of this book. I listened to their comments and used many of them. This book is better because of help from my friends.

Make a plan. Develop an action plan for accomplishing your goals. By their nature, goals are often complex. Accomplishing them takes more than a few steps or actions. List all the things you'll need to do to accomplish your goals. Focus on the critical few things you need to do, not the trivial many. Break your goals into pieces. Set milestones, or mini goals. Accomplishing these milestones will give you the motivation to continue working toward your ultimate goal of career success.

Prepare for the worst. Ask yourself, "What can go wrong?" and "What obstacles am I likely to encounter along the way?" Identify potential problems and make tentative plans for dealing with them before you begin work on your goals. This way, the problems will be less jarring when they happen. You'll be able to take them in your stride and keep moving forward. I knew that unexpected client work, while very welcome, might slow me down on meeting my goal of a first draft by June 30. That's why I set June 30 instead of May 31 as my goal. I was planning for some slippage on my date.

Take action. As the Nike ads say, "Just do it!" You've planned your work, now work your plan. Begin with step one and continue until you've accomplished your goals. I wrote a little every day. I knew I needed to do it to meet my goal.

Adapt. Make adjustments on the fly. As you work toward your goals, focus on making sure that your actions are moving you closer to achieving them. You may find that your plans were off-target. If so, revise them and keep on working.

Reflect. When you've completed all the steps in your plan for a goal, take a minute to reflect. Go back to the first step, your specific and measurable goal. Review the results. Ask yourself if you accomplished what you set out to do. If so, great. If not, consider revising your goal or coming up with a new plan that will get you to your original goal.

Occasionally, meeting your goals can be difficult. Sometimes, you just have to do the best with what you've got. Margaret Wheatley is a fellow alum of the Harvard Graduate School of Education. On the very last page of her wonderful little book *Turning to One Another,* she tells a great story. It comes from the Aztec people of Mexico.

"It is said by our Grandparents that a long time ago there was a great fire in the forests that covered our Earth. People and animals started to run, trying to escape the fire. Our brother owl, Tecolotl, was running away also when he noticed a small bird hurrying back and forth between the nearest river and the fire. He headed towards this small bird.

"He noticed that it was our brother the Quetzal bird, Quetzaltototl, running to the river, picking up small drops of water in his beak, then returning to the fire to throw that tiny bit of water on the flame. Owl approached Quetzal bird and yelled at him: 'What are you doing, brother? Are you stupid? You are not going to achieve anything by doing this. What are you trying to do? You must run for your life!'"

"Quetzal bird stopped for a moment and looked at owl and then answered, 'I am doing the best I can with what I have.'"

"It is remembered by our Grandparents that a long time ago the forests that covered our Earth were saved from a great fire by a small Quetzal bird, an owl and many other animals and people who got together to put out the flames."

I love this story. It illustrates one of my favorite beliefs, the power of one. It also makes excellent point about achieving your goals – do what you can with what you have. Many people miss a deadline and say, "I didn't have all of the information I needed." Those committed to their career success either make sure they get the information or do the best job they can in spite of the missing information.

At Penn State, I studied journalism. Bob Farson was one of my favorite professors. A favorite saying of his was, "Go with what you've got." He always told us that we would probably never have all the information we needed or wanted to write a story, but the deadline was more important than a complete story – "You can't print a blank newspaper or go on the air at 6:00 and say 'give us five minutes to finish getting ready.'" He was right.

People committed to taking personal responsibility for their career success do the best with what they've got. If they don't have what they want or need, they get it. If they can't get it, they do the best they can without it. People who reach their goals don't make excuses. They deliver.

Here is my summary of how to achieve the high goals you set for yourself:

1. Be Decisive

Career success is a choice. Decide what you want, why you want it and how you plan to achieve it. No one else can, will or should do that for you.

2. Stay Focused

Your ability to maintain your focus from beginning to end will determine your outcome, i.e., whether or not you achieve your goals.

3. Welcome Failure

The fundamental question is not whether you should accept failure. You have no choice but to expect it as a temporary condition on the path to career success. Rather, you should anticipate failure and redirect resources to grow from the experience.

4. Write Your Goals

Your mind, while blessed with permanent memory, is cursed with lousy recall. You forget things. Write your goals down.

5. Plan Thoroughly

Planning saves 10 to 1 in execution. Proper planning prevents poor performance.

6. Involve Others

Nobody goes through life alone. Create a "Personal Board of Directors," people whose wisdom, knowledge and character you respect, to help you achieve your goals.

7. Take Purposeful Action

Career success isn't a spectator sport – achievement demands action. You have to do the work necessary to turn your goals into results.

8. Reward Yourself

Rewards work. Give yourself small rewards as you reach milestones. Take time to celebrate when you accomplish a goal. Accomplishing goals is the result of hard work, focus and persistence. Take a minute to recognize and reward yourself for a job well done.

9. Review and Revise Your Plans

Things change. Even the best plans need to change with the

circumstances. No plan holds up against opposition. Review your plans often and revise them as needed. This is your insurance policy on career success.

10. Maintain Your Integrity

Maintain your commitment to career success. Do whatever it takes to achieve your goals. Don't settle for excuses. Maintain the integrity of your goals.

Chapter 6

Stuff Happens; Choose to Respond Positively

I'm always looking for ways to get my common sense message about life and career success across to my coaching clients, the people who read my blog and my books and those on my membership site. That's why I was struck by a passage in Tracy Chevalier's book *Remarkable Creatures*. If you don't know Tracy Chevalier, you should. For my money, she is one of the best novelists writing today. Her first book *Girl With a Pearl Earring* was a mega-bestseller and was made into a movie starring Scarlett Johansson.

In *Remarkable Creatures,* she tells the story of two women fossil hunters in early 19th century England, one a middle-aged spinster, the other, a young girl. Both are committed. Here is how Elizabeth Philpot, the spinster, describes committed fossil hunters…

"Hunters spend hour after hour, day after day, out in all weather, our faces sunburnt, our hair tangled by the wind, our eyes in a permanent squint, our nails ragged and our fingertips torn, our hands chapped. Our boots are trimmed with mud and stained with seawater. Our clothes are filthy by the end of the day. Often we find nothing, but we are patient and hardworking and not put off by coming back empty-handed… Those serious about fossils know their search is never over. There will always be more specimens to discover and study, for, as with people, each fossil is unique. There can never be too many."

I love this passage. In wonderful prose, it describes my thoughts and beliefs on the importance of knowing your purpose in life and committing to it. "Often we find nothing, but we are patient and hardworking and not put off by coming back empty-handed." That's exactly what I'm talking about when I tell my clients, "Stuff happens. The stuff that happens, good or bad, is not what's important. What is important is how you react to it."

Be patient and hardworking. Don't be put off by a day where you come back empty-handed. Choose to believe that your hard work will pay off. Commit to taking personal responsibility for living your life's purpose – whether it is fossil hunting, selling, building things or helping others.

People who commit to taking personal responsibility for creating their life and career success know that their personal quest is never over – there will always be more to do, more to accomplish.

It's been almost 40 years since I first heard about Abraham Maslow's hierarchy of human needs. If you're not familiar with it, Dr. Maslow suggested that all human beings have a series of needs that they strive to satisfy. He arranged these needs in a pyramid. According to his theory, safety is the first and most basic human need. It is at the bottom of the pyramid. We all strive to remain safe in an uncertain world – we all want to live another day.

Security is next. Once we are reasonably sure that we will survive this moment and this day, our needs move to developing a sense of security, one in which we feel that our lives and quality of our lives will remain constant. Sadly, in today's economy and its record unemployment, many people must struggle to meet their security needs.

Affiliation is next. Once we feel safe and secure, we search for meaningful relationships in our lives.

Recognition is next. Once we feel safe, secure and valued by others, we crave recognition—in the form of praise, promotions, more money.

Self-actualization is at the top of the pyramid. Maslow says that after our safety, security, affiliation and recognition needs are satisfied, we turn our attention to what he calls "self-actualization," a state of being all that we can be.

He suggests that we human beings can never be completely self-actualized because as soon as we reach one goal, we realize that there is always something more that we can achieve. Once Bill Gates became one of the world's wealthiest men, he realized that he could be doing more to help others. So he created his foundation.

Once I created and ran a successful consulting practice, I realized that I could do more to share my knowledge about career success with a wider audience. That's why I started writing books and blogging – and why I created the *My Corporate Climb* membership site.

Speaking through a spinster fossil hunter, Tracy Chevalier says, "There will always be more specimens to discover and study, for, as with people, each fossil is unique. There can never be too many." Indeed, there will always be more to do, more to accomplish – if only you clarify your life's purpose and then commit to taking personal responsibility for it.

The common sense point here is simple. Successful people are clear on their purpose and direction in life. They commit to taking personal responsibility for living their life purpose. If you want to achieve career success, you need to do the same. Clarify what you want from your life and career. Then commit to doing whatever it takes to get it. Set high goals. React positively to setbacks, problems and negative people and events. Keep at it. Don't let a day when you come back empty-handed in your quest for career success get you down. Get up the next day with optimism in your heart and keep working toward the mighty purpose you've set for yourself.

Section 3

Build Your
Self-Confidence

I f you want to become self-confident, you need to do three things. First, become an optimist. Learn from and then forget yesterday's mistakes. Focus on tomorrow's achievements. Second, face your fears and take action. Action cures fear. Procrastination and inaction compound it. Failure is rarely fatal. Do something, anything that will move you closer to achieving your goals. Third, surround yourself with positive people. Build a network of supportive friends. Eliminate the negative people from your life. And just as important, find a mentor to help build your confidence and guide you along the way.

Chesley B. "Sully" Sullenberger III is a hero. I'm sure you know by now that in January 2009 he safely landed a US Airways Airbus A320 with 155 passengers and crew on board on the Hudson River. And then he walked the cabin – twice – to make sure no one was on board before he left the aircraft. Everybody survived. It's an amazing story. In one of those coincidences that make life interesting, Doreen Welsh, a high school classmate of mine, was one of the flight attendants on that flight. She and Sully Sullenberger were the last ones out of the plane.

When I watched the news coverage that night, I thought, "There's a man who is totally confident in his skills as a pilot." Self-confidence is an important key to life and career success. That day, Sully Sullenberger was the embodiment of optimism and the willingness to act in the face of fear.

I believe there is one other thing that contributed to Sully's confidence in his ability to land a plane on a river, and that's preparation. Since 1980, he has been a pilot with US Airways. He has trained pilots, helped streamline passenger service, led efforts to improve safety at airports, aided the National Transportation Safety Board in investigating accidents and co-written a technical paper with NASA on crew decision-making errors. Before joining US Airways, he was a fighter pilot. He is a graduate of the Air Force Academy.

He is the former safety chairman of the Air Line Pilots Association and is a visiting scholar at the Center for Catastrophic Risk Management at the University of California, Berkeley, a research center that studies natural and man-made disasters from floods to airplane crashes.

I wouldn't want to be on a plane that had to ditch in a river. If I had to be, though, I'd want Sully Sullenberger to be the pilot. He was as prepared as anyone to do the job.

He was prepared because of his training, more than 40 years' experience as a pilot and his outside work and continuing education. From what I can tell, Sully Sullenberger knows more about flying and decision-making in stressful situations and airplane accidents than anybody else. He was prepared to do something incredibly difficult when the time came. He acted in a calm and confident manner.

We can all take a lesson from him. No matter what you do, the more prepared you are, the more confident you'll be in your ability to handle routine problems and the occasional crisis.

An early mentor used to tell me, "Bud, preparation makes up for a lack of talent." In Sully Sullenberger's case, preparation enhanced his uncommon flying talent.

The common sense point here is simple. Successful people are self-confident. Preparation enhances self-confidence. When you anticipate and mentally rehearse what you'll do in a difficult situation, you'll have the confidence to act swiftly and surely in that situation. Just ask Sully Sullenberger. You can't prepare for every contingency. You can, however, identify problems and opportunities and prepare for them. This will not only improve your confidence, it will improve your performance under pressure.

Chapter 7

Choose Optimism

T here's an old saying, "Optimists are right, pessimists are, too. You get to choose which one you'll be." I choose optimism. Optimism is a great way to create your corporate career success.

When I was young, I participated in the Optimist International annual oratory contest. The topic was "Optimism, Youth's Greatest Asset," something hard enough for a ninth-grader to say (think Joe Pesci in *My Cousin Vinnie*) let alone write and deliver a 10-minute talk on. It was a great experience for me, one that gave me some of the confidence I needed to become a professional speaker.

Optimist International is an outstanding service organization. Its mission is to bring out the best in kids and to help them develop to their full potential by providing hope and positive vision. Their touchstone is the Optimist Creed. It's some of the best common sense advice I've ever read. I have a copy of it posted in my office. Judge for yourself…

The Optimist Creed

Promise Yourself:

- To be so strong that nothing can disturb your peace of mind.
- To talk health, happiness and prosperity to every person you meet.
- To make all your friends feel that there is something in them.
- To look at the sunny side of everything and make your optimism come true.
- To think only of the best, to work only for the best, and to expect only the best.
- To be just as enthusiastic about the success of others as you are about your own.
- To forget the mistakes of the past and press on to the greater achievements of the future.
- To wear a cheerful countenance at all times and give every living creature you meet a smile.
- To give so much time to the improvement of yourself that you have no time to criticize others.
- To be too large for worry, too noble for anger, too strong for fear, and too happy to permit the presence of trouble.

The creed's seventh point – forget the mistakes of the past and press on to the greater achievements of the future – is the most helpful to me. I am an active person. I am always looking for new and better ways to do my work and get across my message. I try new things all the time. Some of the things I try don't work out as planned. I treat these failures as learning experiences. I use them to help me to create greater achievements in the future.

That's what optimists do and what you should do, too. Embrace your mistakes and failures. Learn from them. Treating mistakes and failures as learning opportunities is a great way to jumpstart your life and career success.

If you follow the common sense advice in The Optimist Creed, you'll not only become a more self-confident and optimistic person, you'll become a corporate career success.

I believe in The Optimist Creed so strongly that I have created a pdf of it suitable for framing. If you want a copy to hang in your office or workspace, go to http://budbilanich.com/optimist/.

Self-confidence leads to career success, which leads to increased self-confidence, which leads to higher levels of career success. A nice, positive upward spiral.

You might say, "That's great, Bud, but how do I become self-confident if I'm new in my job or career and haven't had a lot of success to bolster my self-confidence?" There's a saying that applies here: "Fake it till you make it." In other words, act as if you're successful. This will help you succeed. Your successes help build self-confidence.

How do you "fake it till you make it?" Begin with affirmations. If you're in a new job, tell yourself, "I have the skills and desire to succeed in this job," several times a day. Repeat this often enough and you'll begin to believe it. This will help you perform at the level necessary to succeed in your job.

Affirmations are positive self-talk. In an earlier chapter, I mentioned that I named a star after myself to help me become a star in the career success coaching business.

Self-confidence will come with the successes you create from your affirmations. The self-confidence → success → self-confidence cycle is an upward spiral. You have to enter the cycle somewhere. Most of us don't have a strong track record as we begin our careers, move into a new job or start a business. So, you have to "fake it till you make it" by finding ways to bolster your self-confidence until you have some real successes you can build on. Affirmations are a great tool for helping you "fake it till you make it."

Chapter 8

Face Your Fears and Act

"What worries you, masters you." That quote gets to the heart of fear and worry.

Worry is the enemy of career success. Now, I guarantee that you'll worry occasionally. Just don't let it conquer you.

Worry can be useful. If you step off the curb in New York City and a taxi is coming, you had better be worried. But you can't let worry stop you from living your dreams. Drive your worries into a small corner. Take the initiative. Go out and get whatever is out to get you. Push back on whatever is pushing on you.

Worry and fear are enemies of self-confidence. They're also normal, human reactions to difficulties. Indecision and inactivity feed fear and worry but action starves them.

My common sense prescription for dealing with fear and worry is simple. First, identify those things you fear or that cause you to worry. Second, admit you are fearful or worried. Third, accept the fact that some situations make you fearful or worried. Fourth, and most important, confront your fears and worries and take action to overcome them.

In April 1988, I left a secure job with a Fortune 50 company to start my coaching, consulting and speaking business. Was I fearful? Was I worried? You bet I was!

For years, I had talked about being in business for myself, yet I never took the leap because I had never worked through the four steps of dealing with fear and worry.

For years, I hadn't identified the fact that I was afraid of failing in a business venture. Once I identified this – something that took me a long time to admit to myself – I could move past it. I always had considered myself as being self-confident and a bit of a risk-taker. After all, I left a well-paying job at 30 to return to school full time. Other than incurring some debt, there was little risk in choosing graduate school at Harvard. It was a pretty safe thing. Starting a business with a small safety net was risky – and it scared and worried me.

Once I admitted I was scared and worried, I was able to accept fear and worry. This was a good thing because I now had to choose. Do I live with fear and worry that's stopping me from doing something I want to do? Or do I not let fear and worry master me?

I chose the latter. I took action. I quit my job and started a business. They say that "ignorance is bliss." In my case, this certainly was true. I had no idea what it takes to succeed in business on your own. In fact, I've often joked that if I knew what I know

now, I might never have done it.

But that would have meant letting fear and worry triumph. I didn't. I took action. And then worked liked hell to make sure that I would succeed. I drove my fears and worries "into a small corner" by hard work.

I proved to myself that action does help you overcome fear and worry.

Having said all that, let me reiterate: Fear is normal. Fear is common. Fear is human. Fear is also a killer of career success. At times, we're all afraid. Successful people face their fears and act. Over the years, I've learned a few things about fear.

Fear breeds indifference. Indifference breeds self-doubt and worry. Often, it's easier to go with the flow and do nothing than attempt to do something you're afraid of. When you say to yourself, "It's OK, it doesn't really matter anyway," ask the next question – "What am I afraid of?" Identifying your fear is the first step in dealing with it.

Self-doubt is a form of negative self-talk. Our words can become self-fulfilling prophecies. Positive self-talk leads to career success. Negative self-talk leads to fear and failure. If you catch yourself saying, "I can't do this; I'll never be successful; I'll never get out of this mess," you never will. If you say, "I can do this; I have what it takes to succeed; I can solve this problem," you will.

Worry and excessive caution can paralyze you. Some people spend so much time worrying about the bad things that *could* or *might* happen that they never take action and actually do something to prove that good things happen, too. Worrying too much can bring you and your life to a screeching halt.

A boat that never leaves the harbor is safe. That boat, however, is not doing what it is meant to be doing. The same is true for people. If you never take a risk, you'll never know what you are capable of accomplishing.

Fear is the enemy of self-confidence. Self-confident people face their fears and act. Procrastination is the physical manifestation of fear. When I find myself procrastinating, I stop and ask myself, "What are you afraid of here, Bud?"

Usually, the answer is one of the 12 common fears I've listed here. Which stop you from moving forward? What are you doing about them?

1. Fear of failure

This has its roots in the misconception that everything you do has to be 100% successful.

2. Fear of success

This is based on the idea that success is likely to mean more responsibility and attention, coupled with pressure to continue to perform at a high level.

3. Fear of being judged

This fear comes from the need for approval that most people develop in childhood.

4. **Fear of emotional pain**

   This type of fear is rooted in wanting to avoid potential negative consequences of your actions.

5. **Fear of embarrassment**

   This is a result of empowering others to judge you when you demonstrate that you're only human by making mistakes and lapses of judgment.

6. **Fear of being abandoned or being alone**

   This fear is related to rejection and low self-esteem.

7. **Fear of rejection**

   This comes from personalizing what others do and say.

8. **Fear of expressing your true feelings**

   This type of fear holds you back from engaging in open, honest dialogue with the people in your life.

9. **Fear of intimacy**

   This type of fear manifests itself by an unwillingness to let others get too close, lest they discover the "real you."

10. **Fear of the unknown**

    This is a needless worry about all the bad things that could happen if you decide to make a change in your life.

11. Fear of loss

This fear is related to the potential pain associated with no longer having something or someone of emotional significance to you.

12. Fear of death

The ultimate fear of the unknown. What will happen once our spirit leaves our body?

By identifying what you fear, you are more than half-way to conquering it.

Here's a recap of my tips for doing battle with your fears…

Identify what you fear. Figure out why you're afraid. Is it fear of failure? Fear of making the wrong decision? Fear of a lost opportunity? Are you afraid that you aren't up to the task? Once you identify the reason for your fear, you're on your way to overcoming it.

Admit your fears. It's OK to be afraid. You wouldn't be human if you weren't afraid. A definition of courage is the ability to feel fear and still do what you have to do regardless of it. In 1988, I faced a frightening decision. Should I stay in a comfortable, but ultimately unsatisfying job, with a large corporation or should I start a business? I was afraid of failing. Failing meant I would lose my savings and have to start over again looking for a job in another corporation. Once I identified my fear and admitted it, however, I was able to take the next step – acceptance.

Accept your fears. This is important because it shows that you know you're human. Once I accepted my fear of failing, I could start my business and succeed. In fact, I embraced my fear of failure. It made me work harder. It pushed me to work the long hours and learn the entrepreneurship lessons to be successful as a self-employed coach, consultant and speaker.

Take action. Action cures fear. It's the most important of the four steps. Do something! The worst thing that can happen is that you'll find it was the wrong thing to do – and you will have eliminated one thing from your list of possible actions.

Action is the antidote to fear. In most cases, you'll choose wisely and your fears won't be realized. In the cases when you choose poorly, you'll find that failure isn't as catastrophic as you imagined. Successful people learn from failure. By acting on your fears, you win on both counts. You win if you make a good decision and things work out. You win if you make a bad decision and things go poorly because it's an opportunity to learn from your decision and its subsequent problems.

Chapter 9

Surround Yourself With Positive People

Successful people surround themselves with positive people – those who are positive by nature and positive about their life and career success. Positive people are optimistic. As I mentioned earlier, optimism is the first step in building self-confidence.

Positive people make you feel good about yourself because they feel good about themselves and life in general. They help you build self-esteem because they have a strong sense of self-esteem. Positive people are there when you doubt yourself. They aren't threatened by you or your success. They know that self-esteem and career success are part of a big pie, and there's enough of the pie to go around. Positive people give away self-esteem and help others create their career success. You can build your self-confidence and jumpstart your career success just by being around upbeat, positive people.

Joining or forming a mastermind group is a great way to surround yourself with positive people. While it's a common term today, to the best of my knowledge, Napoleon Hill was the first person to use the term "mastermind group" in his timeless work *Think and Grow Rich*.

The idea behind a mastermind group is simple. No one person has sufficient experience, knowledge and ability to succeed in this life without the cooperation of others. When you're creating your success plan, it helps to get the input and thinking of as many people as possible. Remember, surrounding yourself with positive people is a good way to build your self-confidence and to create the life and career success you want and deserve.

Entrepreneurs often form mastermind groups to exchange ideas on how to grow their businesses. I believe that everybody can benefit from being part of a mastermind group. You can form a mastermind group with friends where you work or with friends from church or synagogue – or just friends you meet at your kids' sporting events. It doesn't matter. Just find a like-minded group of people who want to succeed in their lives and careers and who are willing to help you succeed in return for your helping them succeed.

Here are a few ideas for forming a mastermind group…

- Mastermind with people you like and who share your interests and goals. If you don't feel the mastermind group is discussing things that are relevant to you, you're probably in the wrong group. That's OK. Just leave and find another group of people who are aligned with your thinking and your life and career success goals. This is less of a problem if you take the initiative to create your own mastermind group.

- Meet in person if you can. In the best mastermind groups, people are comfortable with and like and trust one other. This comfort, affection and trust comes with the personal connection.
- Meet frequently – at least once a month. Every two weeks is even better. Frequent meetings create momentum, which will create personal accountability and drive.
- Make sure everyone gets a chance to speak and have his or her ideas reviewed by the group. Some mastermind groups designate a timer to keep things on track. You can't have one member dominate the meetings while others don't get a chance to get the benefit of the group's thinking.
- I find it best not to add new members once the group has been formed. If someone leaves the group, you may consider inviting another member to join. If you do, make sure it is a decision endorsed by the entire group. In effective mastermind groups, a sense of cohesion develops quickly. You can hamper this cohesion by adding just one member.
- Care as much about the career success of the other members of the group as you do about your own. Keep the sixth point of The Optimist Creed in mind – "Be just as enthusiastic about the success of others as you are about your own" – as you meet with the mastermind group.

When it comes to creating the life and career success that you want and deserve, two heads or three heads or six heads are better than one head. That's why forming or joining a mastermind group is a good idea. Mastermind groups are not just for entrepreneurs. We can all benefit from the thinking of others. Others can benefit from our thinking.

A word to the wise. Your mastermind group will work for you, only if you are willing to work for it. A mastermind group is a two-way street. The more you put into helping others, the more others will put into helping you. When you get into a mastermind group, don't keep score. I wrote Rule # 2 in *42 Rules for Creating WE*: There Is No Quid Pro Quo in WE. This kind of thinking applies to mastermind groups. Be willing to listen and share your advice first – with no expectation of return. Ironically, if you do this, you'll get a lot in return. I guarantee it.

Here's another story about the power of positive people. Not long ago, I did a talk for a local real estate company. This was at the height of the subprime mortgage crisis, not a good time to be in the real estate business. As people entered the room, most came over and asked if I was the speaker and then introduced themselves. This was great because it put me at ease. Once I knew their names, it was easier to relax and enjoy giving my talk.

As the moderator kicked off the session, she recognized several people in attendance who got a round of applause for their accomplishments. When she introduced me, the audience also applauded. While I spoke, I could see people taking notes and nodding their heads. All of which made it easier to connect to them as an audience and to do a better job on my talk. In short, my self-confidence was buoyed by the positive energy I observed before and during the talk.

I am a professional speaker. I do lots of speeches. I still get nervous before each one. I welcome these nerves because I know they're the body's way of telling me that I'm up for the presentation. I worry when I'm not a little nervous. To me, that indicates that I might be a little flat during the talk.

Because people introduced themselves before my talk, I knew this was a positive audience. Even though I had the butterflies, my nerves were in check and my self-confidence high because of the positive energy in the room.

When I got to the part about surrounding yourself with positive people, everyone nodded. They got it – they knew exactly what I was talking about. Afterwards, a few people came up to me to discuss that very point. They said that being in the company of positive people was one of the most important aspects of their success.

This is a small example but a telling one. To succeed in sales, you have to be self-confident. By its nature, selling involves rejection. It takes a self-confident person to make the sixth call after getting nowhere on the previous five. Successful salespeople face and deal with their fears of rejection. And they seek out positive people to help them stay motivated to keep doing what it takes to succeed.

This is important in other aspects of life as well. The people around you have an amazing impact on your view of life. When you surround yourself with negative or cynical people, you become negative and cynical. On the other hand, when you surround yourself with positive, self-confident people, you become positive and self-confident.

The choice is yours. I choose to surround myself with positive people. Not only do they help my self-confidence, they're more fun to be around.

Here's another interesting story about surrounding yourself with positive people. It comes from Sherman Alexie's novel *The Absolutely True Diary of a Part-Time Indian*. The protagonist is a young Native American boy who leaves the reservation to attend school in an all-white school district. Check it out…

"Something magical happened to me when I went to Reardon. Overnight I became a good player.

I suppose it had something to do with confidence. In Reardon my coach and the other players wanted me to be good. They needed me to be good. They expected me to be good. And so, I became good.

I wanted to live up to expectations. I guess that's what it comes down to. The power of expectations. And as they expected more of me, I expected more of myself, and it just grew and grew until I was scoring twelve points a game – as a freshman."

The coach wanted him to guard the other team's best player in a very important game.

"'Coach,' I said, 'I don't think I can do it.' He walked over to me, kneeled, and pushed his forehead against mine. Our eyes were like an inch apart. I could smell cigarettes and chocolate on his breath.

'You can do it,' Coach said. 'You can do it,' Coach said again. He didn't shout it. He whispered it, like a prayer. And he kept whispering again. Until the prayer turned into a song. And then, for some magical reason, I believed him…

'I can do it,' I said to Coach, to my teammates, to the world.

'You can do it,' Coach said. 'I can do it.' 'You can do it.' 'I can do it.'

Do you know how amazing it is to hear that from anybody? It's one of the simplest sentences in the world, just four words, but they're the four hugest words in the world when they're put together.

'You can do it.'

'I can do it.'

'Let's do it…'"

As I read those words, I could see that locker room and feel the excitement – not only on Coach's part and the part of the young Native American, but the entire team. We all need people like Coach in our lives. That's why it's so important to surround yourself with positive people. When you find people who believe in you and tell you "you can do it," you begin to believe in yourself.

As Sherman Alexie says, "I wanted to live up to expectations. I guess that's what it comes down to – the power of expectations. And as they expected more of me, I expected more of myself, and it just grew and grew…."

Self-confident people surround themselves with positive people. Positive people will expect a lot of you and from you. These expectations will help you become a more confident person. Never underestimate the power of positive people. They will help your confidence and get you on the path to your corporate career success. Befriend all the positive people you can. Hold them close. Treasure them and their friendship. They can help you achieve your dreams.

A couple of years ago, I did a blog post on optimism and self-confidence. I mentioned a quote in which someone named Ambrose Bierce bashed optimism. "The doctrine that everything is beautiful, including what is ugly, everything good, especially the bad, and everything right that is wrong... It is hereditary, but fortunately not contagious."

The other day, I came across another quote from Bierce: "Calamities are of two kinds: misfortunes to ourselves, and good fortune to others." I found these quotes to be really cynical, so I decided to learn something about Ambrose Bierce. As it turns out, he was called "Bitter Bierce" by his contemporaries. And I can see why. First he bashes optimism and then he suggests that human beings see the good fortune of others as a personal calamity.

Ambrose Bierce is an interesting character. He was born in 1842 and served in the Union Army during the Civil War. No one knows for sure but it is thought that he died in 1914. In 1913, he traveled to Mexico to observe firsthand the revolution going on there.

He joined Pancho Villa's army in Juarez. On December 26, 1913, he posted a letter to a friend from the city of Chihuahua. That was his last correspondence. Wikipedia says, "Several writers have speculated that he headed north to the Grand Canyon, found a remote spot there and shot himself, though no evidence exists to support this view. All investigations into his fate have proved fruitless, and despite an abundance of theories, his end remains shrouded in mystery. The date of his death is generally cited as '1914?'" His disappearance is one of the most famous in American literary history.

In 1906, he published *The Cynic's Word Book* later known as *The Devil's Dictionary*. It is a book of satirical definitions of English words. Bierce was clever, I'll give him that. I often see quotes from this book online, including the one that inspired today's post, "Calamities are of two kinds: misfortunes to ourselves, and good fortune to others."

But I digress. I wish he were around today because I would like to ask him where he got his bleak view of human nature. He defines politeness as, "The most acceptable hypocrisy." In another quote, he defines perseverance as, "A lowly virtue whereby mediocrity achieves an inglorious success."

Do you know any people like Ambrose Bierce? If you do, hold them at arm's length. While you may find them to be witty and entertaining at first, they will drag you down in the long run.

People like Ambrose Bierce may be clever but their views are incompatible with becoming self-confident. Self-confident people look for, and often find, the best in others. They are polite because it is the best way to build strong relationships. They are willing to extend themselves to help others, even when they can see no immediate return.

You know I am a fan of The Optimist Creed. Point 6 says,

"Promise yourself to be just as enthusiastic about the success of others as you are of your own."

This is 180 degrees from the Ambrose Bierce quote I cited earlier and from his views in general. Self-confident, optimistic people aren't jealous or upset by the success of others. They are pleased when others succeed. They use others' success as an inspiration to motivate themselves to achieve bigger and better successes.

The common sense point here is clear. Successful people are self-confident and interpersonally competent. They build strong relationships with the people around them. In part, they build these relationships by being genuinely pleased about the success of others. They are neither jealous nor petty. They are happy to see others succeed. Self-confident and interpersonally competent people use the success of others to motivate themselves to greater success.

Chapter 10

Find a Mentor to Help You Grow and Succeed

The term "mentor" comes from *The Odyssey*. Before he set out to fight the Trojan War, Odysseus entrusted the care of his son Telemachus to Mentor. The best mentors will help you learn and grow by sharing their knowledge and wisdom. And you benefit from their experience without suffering the consequences of that experience firsthand.

By definition, mentors are positive people. It takes a positive person to give of themselves to help another learn, grow and succeed.

I have been fortunate to have had several mentors in my life and career. All shared key characteristics. They all…

- Were willing to share their wisdom, knowledge, skills.

- Had a positive outlook on life. They helped me through tough times and showed me how to find the opportunity in the difficulties I was facing.
- Were genuinely concerned about me and my success. Besides being knowledgeable, they were empathic.
- Knew what they were doing. I respected them for their knowledge and skills.
- Kept growing themselves. They were curious and inquisitive. Sometimes, the roles were reversed. They asked what I was reading and then read the books themselves – so they could learn and we could discuss the ideas.
- Gave me direct, constructive feedback. They held me to high standards. They congratulated me when I met their expectations. They corrected me when I failed to do so – but in a way where I learned what not to do the next time.
- Earned the respect of colleagues. People highly regarded in their field or company make the best mentors.
- Sought out and valued the opinions of others. My best mentor always told me to listen carefully to the people I disagreed with – so I might learn something. He was right.

As the saying goes, a mentor is someone whose hindsight can become your foresight.

Do you want to find a mentor? Just look around you. Who are the people you admire and want to emulate? Watch what they do and do the same. I've had mentors who didn't realize they were mentoring me.

I learned how to build a network of solid contacts by watching

Maggie Watson. I learned the rules of business etiquette and dressing for success by watching Bill Rankin. I learned how to become a first-rate public speaker by watching Steve Roesler. I learned how to become a trusted advisor by watching Don Nelson. I learned how to carry myself with dignity in even the most difficult situations by watching JF and Carol Kiernan. I learned how to become a better conversationalist by watching my wife Cathy.

The reverse is also true. I've learned plenty about what not to do to build self-esteem, give performance feedback and treat people with respect and dignity from observing a few of my managers over the years.

I've found that if you want to have an acknowledged mentoring relationship, all you have to do is ask. Go to the people you admire and tell them that you admire their judgment and would like to learn from them. Ask if you can impose on their time to get answers to questions you have. I have never had anyone turn me down when I've asked this way.

I've created a mentor acronym. Look for these qualities in people you want to mentor you. A good mentor…

M Motivates you to accomplish more than you think you can.

E Expects the best from you.

N Never gives up on you or lets you give up on yourself.

T Tells you the truth – even when it hurts.

O Occasionally kicks your butt.

R Really cares about you and your success.

Chapter 11

Mentor Others

J ust as it's important to find someone to mentor you, it's important to mentor others. You don't have to be in a formal leadership position or have years and years of experience to mentor someone else. It's never too early to become a mentor. We all have something to give and the sooner you begin giving, the better. If you're in college, you can mentor high school students. If you're a recent graduate, you can mentor those still in school.

I take great pleasure in mentoring others. I love it when I can use my experience to help accelerate someone else's growth. It takes the sting out of some of the negative consequences I've experienced because of poor judgment. I think to myself "At least he or she won't have to go through that."

In his book *Love is the Killer App* Tim Sanders tells the story of how he turned one of the people who worked for him from a "mad dog" into a "love cat." The advice is simple: "Offer your wisdom freely… And always be human."

Tim is spot on. Mentoring is a great way to become a love cat by

serving others. The more you serve others, the more confidence –
and corporate career success – will come your way. Besides that,
you'll grow by mentoring. As you reflect on your life experiences
and distill them into nuggets you can share, your knowledge
becomes wisdom. You'll be better able to help others learn and
grow and be able to take full advantage of what you know. You
never learn something so completely as when you teach it.

Any mentoring relationship needs to focus on the one being
mentored. Mentoring someone will almost always be a satisfying
experience for you. Remember, though, that it's not about you – it's
about others. Accept them for who they are. Help them proceed at
their own pace. The best mentoring relationships are guided by the
persons being mentored.

Mentoring should be a positive experience for everyone
involved. You need to avoid treating the person you are mentoring
as incompetent or incapable. Rather, think of him or her as
someone who lacks experience and who needs guidance. Don't
criticize. Help the other person think through the consequences of
a behavior and to identify more positive ways of handling difficult
or troubling situations.

Hold the persons you mentor responsible for their success. Give
them small assignments. Don't let them off the hook if they fail to
complete them. Be willing to give of yourself and your time and
make sure the person you mentor does, too.

Recognize that the relationship will end. If you've done a good
job, the person you are mentoring will need to move on at some
point. It's part of the cycle. It can be hard to let go but you can feel

good about seeing someone move on to bigger and better things – and another mentor.

Remember my mentor acronym. A good mentor…

M Motivates you to accomplish more than you think you can.
E Expects the best of you.
N Never gives up on you or lets you give up on yourself.
T Tells you the truth, even when it hurts.
O Occasionally kicks your butt.
R Really cares about you and your success.

Besides looking for people with these qualities when searching for a mentor, make sure you embody them yourself when mentor others.

Section 4

Become an Outstanding Performer

 All successful people are outstanding performers. It's the price of admission to the success club. Don't make the mistake of thinking that performance alone will get you where you want to be. Performance is only one of the seven characteristics of successful people. It's important but alone doesn't guarantee success.

There are several common sense points associated with outstanding performance. Outstanding performance is critical to career and life success. You can't succeed if you're not an outstanding performer. You need to do four things to become an outstanding performer. First, become a lifelong learner. Keep learning and growing. You'll be surprised at how much there is to learn about business and life. Second, develop your business acumen. Learn as much as you can about your company, its competitors and the industry. Third, set high goals – and then meet or exceed them. Use milestones to break your goals into manageable chunks. This way, they'll be easier to achieve. Fourth, get organized. This helps you manage your life, time and stress. Figure out an organizing system that works for you and stick with it.

Louis Pasteur, who invented pasteurization, is considered the father of modern microbiology. I like what he has to say about high performance: "Let me tell you the secret that has led me to my goal: my **strength** lies solely in my **tenacity**."

Here's a story about a tenacious person who is very close to me.

My wife is a volunteer reading tutor at one of Denver's public schools. Cathy has been doing this for several years. She enjoys the children and believes she is making a difference through her volunteer work.

As August turns into September, she always gets excited about another school year and another group of kids. This past year, the school where she volunteers lost its Volunteer Program Coordinator so they were a little slow getting volunteer assignments made.

This didn't stop Cathy. She made a few phone calls to the school asking when they wanted her to begin. She got some vague promises but nothing definite. Finally, she went to the school and basically arranged her own assignment. As usual, she loved the kids and was happy to be back at "her school."

The point of the Pasteur quote and Cathy's tenacity in her volunteer work is simple. Outstanding performers are tenacious in pursuit of goals. They do what it takes to be successful. In Cathy's case, it took driving to the school and being willing to seem like a bit of a pain to an administrator. She was willing to do it because her desire to succeed as a reading volunteer was strong. The third-graders she works with are better for it.

The Dalai Lama has some interesting things to say about outstanding performance and hard work. "One can be deceived by three types of laziness: the laziness of indolence, which is the wish to procrastinate; the laziness of inferiority, which is doubting your capabilities; and the laziness that is attached to negative actions, or putting great effort into non-virtue."

This quote drives home an important point about personal

responsibility and outstanding performance. The Dalai Lama doesn't let us off the hook by saying, "I didn't think I could do it." Instead, he says that doubting our abilities is a form of laziness. That's some tough love!

And he is right. All too often, we let ourselves off the hook by saying, "I'm not going to try that because I don't think I can do it." This is being lazy.

"I can't do it so I won't even try." As I read these words out loud, they sound pretty lame. Agree? If you do, you'll stop using lack of self-confidence as an excuse for not doing the work it takes to become an outstanding performer.

Chapter 12

Become a Lifelong Learner

Outstanding performers are technically competent because they are lifelong learners. I believe that my love of learning and my lifelong pursuit of knowledge are the keys to my life and career success. I'm always learning and always welcome opportunities to learn new things – whether related to my work or not.

You probably have spent a lot of time in college – maybe graduate school, too. You might be tempted to think that you needn't keep learning. After all, isn't learning what you need to know to function in the world of work the point of going to college? Not really. You learn just the basics in college.

Your education really begins when you start working. Thomas Carlyle said, "What we become depends on what we read after all of the professors have finished with us. The greatest university of all is a collection of books."

Carlyle lived in the 19th century. If he were alive today, he might have amended his statement to read, "The Internet is the greatest university of all." It's true. So many of the great books, as well as other career and life success information, are available online. The important thing is to keep learning – how you do it and where you get your information is secondary.

When I speak to graduating college students, I always tell them that the best thing about graduating from college is that you finally get a chance to begin learning – for yourself, not your professors. I have a huge collection of books on a variety of subjects. I turn to them first when I need information to post on my blog, when I'm working with my executive coaching clients, preparing a speech or designing a training program. If I don't find what I want or need in my books, I Google it.

The half-life of knowledge is getting shorter and shorter. If you don't keep learning, you won't keep up. You'll fall behind in the knowledge you need to become an outstanding performer.

As you've probably guessed, my best common sense suggestion for becoming a lifelong learner is simple. Read. Read technical journals. Read trade magazines. Read business publications like *The Wall Street Journal*, *Business Week*, *Fortune* and *Forbes* magazines. If you think they're too stodgy, read *Fast Company*. Read your company's annual report. Read your competitors' annual reports. Read the local newspaper and *The New York Times*. Read news magazines like *Newsweek* and *Time*. Read business and industry blogs. Read books. Reading is the best way to keep up on what's happening in business, your industry and the world.

There are other things you can do to keep learning. Attend seminars. Join the major groups or trade associations for your industry. Attend their meetings and participate. Volunteer for committee work. Become known locally in your field. Take a class at a college or university. Use your company's tuition reimbursement benefit to earn a master's degree.

If you want to become a corporate career success, your education never stops. There are many ways to keep learning. Decide which works for you and then follow through.

Chapter 13

Develop Your Business Acumen

I hear it a couple of times a week. One of my clients says, "I didn't get the promotion I wanted. When I asked why, I was told that I'm not strategic enough." That can be a catch-all phrase to explain away why another candidate was chosen over you. Often it has no real meaning. On the other hand, not being strategic, not demonstrating that you see and understand the big picture, can be an impediment to your corporate climb. As you move up the corporate ladder, you have to become more strategic. You need to develop your business acumen.

Think of business acumen in two ways. First, you have to have a basic understanding of how your company makes money. This means that you have to have a working knowledge of finance, marketing, sales and operations. Second, you have to use this to make sound decisions that contribute to the company's profitability.

In other words, you need to see your company's big picture and how what you do every day contributes to it.

Even if you're in a specialized field like technical support or human resources, you have to understand how business works. You need high technical acumen – the knowledge of your field. You also need to know and understand how your company competes in the marketplace. You may be a technical specialist but you have to be a business generalist.

Business acumen allows you to understand your company's overall strategy and how the company competes in the marketplace. It helps you speak the language of business. This lets you communicate with senior leaders in your company and show them that you're aware of the issues they deal with daily. Developing business acumen shows others that you're a business generalist, not a specialist – an important key to climbing the corporate ladder.

If you Google "business acumen," you'll find five drivers essential to all businesses: Cash, Profits, Assets, Growth and Customers.

Cash is an item on your company's balance sheet that reports the value of its assets that are cash or can be converted into cash immediately. Cash is a company's most liquid asset.

Profits, sometimes called margin, are the money left over after you pay your expenses. Two types of profit, gross and net, are often calculated. Gross profit or margin is your sales minus the cost of goods sold – how much it costs you to develop, make, market, sell and deliver your products. Net profits are gross profits minus expenses and taxes.

Assets are things like company property, equipment and cash. People are listed as an asset on a company's balance sheet but they play a crucial role in how well your company uses its assets. Velocity is a term often applied to assets. The better a company's ability to use its assets to make money, the higher the velocity. The big question here is, "How fast does a company use its assets to increase its profits?"

Growth is typically measured in three ways: Sales, Net Profits and Earnings per Share. If you work for a publicly traded company, your CEO is probably most concerned with earnings per share because that determines the market value of your stock.

Customers are the end users of your company's products and services. Strong companies are good at exceeding customer expectations and in anticipating their needs.

These business drivers are interdependent. Acting on one will have an impact on at least one of the others. For example, if you choose to conserve cash by not investing in new technologies, you might hinder growth because your current technologies are not adequate to increase your market share.

On the other hand, discounting your products may lead to higher sales and improved market share but have a negative impact on your gross margin.

I downloaded a presentation by Kevin Cope, CEO of Acumen Learning, called "What Your CEO Wants You To Know." He suggests that one way to test your business acumen is to see if you can answer 11 questions by reading and studying your company's annual report.

For the most recent fiscal year end:

1. How much cash was on hand?
2. How much cash was generated from operating activities?
3. What was total net income?
4. What was the net profit margin?
5. What were total sales?
6. What was the inventory turnover rate?
7. What was the return on assets?
8. How much did sales grow over the previous year?
9. How much did net income grow over the previous year?
10. How much did Earnings per Share grow over the previous year?
11. How do all of the above compare to your competition?

I know this can sound overwhelming. But the answers to these questions are in your company's annual report. If you don't know how to read the annual report, I suggest you make friends with a few of your finance people. Take them to lunch and ask them to give you a little tutorial on reading an annual report. Trust me, this lunch will be one of the better investments you make in your corporate climb.

It's important to understand how your company makes money by integrating the five drivers. As I've mentioned, the drivers are interdependent. When you do something that has an impact on one, you affect the others. Great companies are good at integrating all five drivers.

But remember, your department or function is likely to emphasize only one or two of the drivers. If you want to be known as someone who understands the big picture, figure out what drivers other departments and functions focus on. In conversations with those from other areas of the company, be aware of what is important to them.

Besides understanding the five business drivers and your company's balance sheet, these simple, common sense steps can help you develop business acumen…

- Schedule a meeting with your manager. Tell him or her you would like to develop a better understanding of your company and how it makes money. Have a discussion about how your department – and you – can make a more significant and positive impact on the business as a whole.
- Figure out the key metrics the senior leaders in your company are focused on. Make sure you know how your role and what you do every day contributes to these metrics.
- Begin to think in terms of how you can impact key metrics. Suggest some projects you can do that will improve the company's performance in one or more of the key metrics.
- Constantly ask yourself, "How can I make a positive impact on the driver or drivers associated with my work? How can I demonstrate measureable results?"
- Start with small, simple steps. As your business acumen develops, you'll be better able to understand and contribute to the big picture – and move your corporate climb along.

To sum up, you demonstrate business acumen and ability to be strategic by doing the following things. Show that you understand how the various areas of your company work together to provide value. Make decisions based on data, not just your intuition. Choose the course of action that will have the best results for the entire company, not just your department. Take calculated risks. Don't choose the first and most obvious answer. Instead, look for unique and creative solutions to problems. Collaborate with others in departments outside yours. Always keep finances in mind when you make decisions. Be persistent and agile. Get the projects done, no matter what obstacles pop up along the way.

Chapter 14

Manage Your Time, Life and Stress

I f you're like most people, you have more to do than time to do it in. I'm good at managing time but I do get stressed and overwhelmed occasionally. Time is a precious, non-renewable resource. When a moment is gone, it's gone forever.

In *The 7 Habits of Highly Effective People*, Stephen Covey presents a time management framework. It goes something like this. When you think of your time, all activities fit into one of four categories:

- Not Important and Not Urgent
- Not Important and Urgent
- Important and Urgent
- Important and Not Urgent

Unfortunately, many people spend a lot of time engaged in not important and not urgent activities. Surfing the web is one of the biggest culprits here. I am pretty disciplined yet I can get caught up following interesting links when I am researching something on the Internet. Following links after you've found what you're looking for is a not important and not urgent activity. It's a waste of time and a productivity killer.

Not important and urgent activities can become time traps. These are the kinds of things that you have to do, but in the greater scheme of things, they aren't likely to do much for your corporate career success. These are things like expense reports and weekly staff meetings – things you have to do but don't contribute to your larger goal. Get them done in a timely manner but don't spend a lot of time at them.

I'm sure you get bombarded with tasks that are not important but urgent. Often these come from your boss. Read the cartoon strip *Dilbert* for a week to see what I mean. It's difficult to refuse many of these tasks. People who manage their time well, however, have the ability to do so.

When I am faced with such a task, I always say, "I was planning on doing this today. I am happy to drop what I was doing and work on your request. I want you to know, though, that I'll have to push back the completing of the other project." Sometimes, my bosses have said, "That's fine." On other occasions, they instructed me to focus on the urgent task that seems unimportant to me.

Here's an example. Many years ago, I was working for a large company in the Training and Development Department. I was designing the curriculum for a sales manager workshop. My boss's boss said to me, "We have some important visitors from Japan here today. I would like you to join them for lunch." I was zoned in on the training design. I didn't want to spend two and a half hours at lunch with guests. So I told him that I was working on the sales manager curriculum design and asked to be excused from the lunch. He told me that it was important for us to be good hosts and that I should make time for the lunch – so I did. Urgent, but not important, won the day. And the reality of everyday life in most companies is that it often does. But that doesn't mean you shouldn't try to avoid it as much as possible.

Important and urgent activities are just what they seem. I write a blog five days a week. Check it out at www.BudBilanich.com. My blog is a marketing tool. It increases my awareness in a crowded market. It positions me as an expert. And it reinforces my Common Sense Guy brand. Writing and posting my blog is an important and urgent activity. It's important because of the reasons I've stated. It's urgent because I have committed to my readers to do it every day. I do it first thing each day. I'm sure that you have several important and urgent activities on your to-do list, too. Do them and do them well.

Important but not urgent activities are where you get the real corporate career success payoff. For example, it's important to become a lifelong learner. That's why you need to read, join professional organizations and volunteer for projects in your company. You probably don't need to read every day and join all the professional organizations in your field and industry. These activities are just not that urgent. You do have to make time for them over the long run. If you don't, you'll find that you're falling behind, not getting ahead or standing still.

Another example – my books serve much the same purpose as

my blog. They increase my awareness in a crowded market, position me as an expert and reinforce my brand. Writing books is an important but not urgent task for me. I manage it by budgeting at least three hours a week to write. As one book goes into the editing and production process, I get busy writing another. This way, I never find myself without a forthcoming book.

It can be hard to budget time for important but not urgent activities because they are, well, not urgent. These activities, however, left unattended soon become important and urgent and may even become career crises. My best advice is to focus on your personal set of important but not urgent activities and build time into your daily or weekly schedule to work on them.

Stress is a thief of productivity and can really get in the way of managing your time. You need to be healthy and alert to perform at your best. I've been collecting health tips for some time and have decided to share some of them – on getting enough sleep and managing stress – with you here.

Get a good night's sleep...

- If possible, go to bed and get up at the same time every day. This will help you regulate your body's internal clock.
- Come up with a bed-time routine to help you relax. Take a bath or read. Listening to classical or new age music helps you fall asleep probably because your body rhythms match the music and it slows your heart rate.
- Avoid stimulants like caffeine and nicotine from late afternoon on. A cup of coffee after dinner may be satisfying

but it's also likely to keep you awake.

- Don't use alcohol to help you sleep. Its sedative effect will wear off and will trigger wakefulness.
- Exercise during the day. It helps you fall asleep quicker at night.

Massage away your stress....

- Massage your scalp. Place your thumbs behind your ears and spread your fingers on top of your head. Make circles with your fingertips.
- Close your eyes and place your ring fingers under your eyebrows near the bridge of your nose. Slowly increase the pressure for five seconds, then release gently. Do this three or four times.
- Place your left hand on the right side of your neck, near your shoulder. Press firmly into the shoulder muscle while tucking your chin into your chest. Hold this position for 10 seconds. Do it again from the other side.
- Lace your fingers together, leaving your thumbs free. Knead your left thumb into the palm of your right hand for 20 to 30 seconds. Do the same for the other hand.

Get a second wind at work...

- Snack on fiber-rich foods such as dried apricots, celery sticks, apples or pistachio nuts. The fiber helps control the release of glucose into your blood stream, preventing energy dips.

- Take a few minutes every few hours to breathe deeply. This will calm you and help you become more mentally focused.
- Go to the rest room and splash cold water on your face.
- Pop a breath mint, as mint flavors are stimulating.
- Take a "good news" inventory at the end of the day. Write down all of the good things that happened. This will energize you for the next day and help you sleep.

Stress can rob you of your productivity. Sleep reenergizes you. Make sure that you get enough. Small self-massages of your head, neck and hands can help you relieve tension. Get your second wind at work by taking a few minutes for yourself every couple of hours.

I find that the Serenity Prayer helps when I am feeling stressed. If you're not familiar with the serenity prayer, it is elegant in its simplicity and wisdom.

> "God grant me the serenity to accept the things I cannot change, courage to change the things I can, and the wisdom to know the difference."

I once saw a blog post by Laura Ries on Success Television.com. Laura listed 99 reasons she says the Serenity Prayer. I'd like to share them with you here. Some will make you smile, some will make you laugh, some will make you cry.

1. A sunny day
2. A rainy day
3. Getting to work on time
4. Being stuck in traffic
5. Waking up late
6. Tossing and turning all night
7. A good night's sleep
8. The flu going around
9. Spring flowers
10. A friend getting married
11. A brand new baby
12. A heart condition
13. Kidney failure
14. Sudden death
15. C-section
16. Hours of labor
17. Dementia
18. Distinguished leader award
19. High school graduation
20. Grand babies
21. Browsing the library
22. Divorce
23. Cheating
24. A job well done
25. Differing values
26. Smiles
27. Twinkling eyes
28. A good laugh
29. Brilliant sunsets
30. Fall colors
31. Grandma's quilt
32. 22-year-old suicide
33. Social injustice
34. Child support arrears
35. Scoliosis
36. Chronic ear infections
37. BS degree
38. MBA
39. Sharing good news
40. Sharing bad news
41. Good friends
42. Not so good friends
43. Betrayal
44. Trust
45. Places that look like picture postcards
46. The house looking like a tornado hit it
47. House full of kids, love and laughter
48. Empty nest
49. Retirement

50. Fluffy pillows
51. Clean clothes
52. Forgiving someone
53. Taking a stand
54. Taking a nap
55. Having money
56. Taking a risk
57. Winning a game
58. Losing a game
59. Starting over
60. Starting over, again
61. Letting go
62. Holding on
63. Solving a puzzle
64. Holding hands
65. Anticipation
66. Friends moving
67. Meeting new people
68. Spending time in a sacred place
69. After-effects of a storm
70. New building
71. Making ice cream
72. Old, forgotten memories
73. Snow ball fights
74. Incontinence
75. Pillow fights
76. Fireworks
77. Car wrecks
78. College shootings
79. Genocide
80. Playing in the rain
81. First dates
82. First day of school
83. Graduation
84. New beginnings
85. Birthday cake
86. Favorite meal
87. Purring cat
88. HPV
89. Broken heart
90. Watching your child sleep
91. Watching your child play
92. Hospitals
93. Job interviews
94. On the job training
95. Mended heart
96. New day
97. Virgin snow
98. Kids growing up so fast
99. HOPE

Laura's grandfather suffers from dementia. She says, "Some days I fight against the things I cannot change. I cannot change that dementia is slowly taking away my grandfather. And I hate that. And I struggle. Then I look for the blessing, and I keep looking until I find it. Otherwise, I'd lose sight of the good things in life. Grandpa is here, he is sharing the stories of his life we never knew. This is reminding me to share with my children stories they have never heard about me as well. My children are going with me to visit Grandpa, and that is a blessing as well."

What are some things in your life you can change? What are some things you cannot? Can you find a place where letting what is, is OK? Are you making the changes that you can?

You can't become an outstanding performer if you can't manage your time, life and stress. Stress happens when you feel out of control. You can't control everything that happens to you. You can control how you react to things that happen to you. If you decide to "accept the things you cannot change, and change the things you can," your stress levels will go down as you work to become an outstanding performer and create the career and life success you want and deserve.

Chapter 15

Live a
Healthy Lifestyle

You have to be in reasonable shape if you want to become a corporate career success. A reasonable level of fitness will help you deal with the inevitable stress that accompanies creating a successful life and career. Diet and exercise are the keys to living a healthy lifestyle. You don't have to be a fitness fanatic. You do need to exercise and pay attention to what you eat.

When it comes to a healthy lifestyle, I'm not the best role model. I've battled weight all my life. As I've grown older, though, I've become more serious about living a healthy lifestyle. I exercise more and pay attention to what I eat.

I have found that the federal government's revised food pyramid is a great guide to eating healthy. I try to follow these guidelines. If you follow them, you will be doing well from a nutrition standpoint. Here are some of its highlights…

Eat at least three ounces of whole grain bread, cereals, crackers, rice or pasta each day. Look for the word "whole" before the grain name on the list of ingredients.

Eat lots of vegetables each day. I'm lucky here. I love vegetables – even brussels sprouts. Dark green and orange vegetables are the best for you. Dry beans and peas are also good for you.

Fruit is good for you, raw fruit is the best. On the other hand, it's best to limit your intake of fruit juice. It's often high in calories and sugar.

Milk is a great source of calcium – something we all need for strong bones. Whole milk is high in fat so it's best to drink low-fat or fat-free milk. Yogurt and cheese are good sources of calcium.

Eat protein (meat, fish and poultry) in small quantities. But bake, broil or grill – don't fry – it.

The Mayo Clinic suggests eating at least three fruits, four vegetables, four to eight servings of grains and pasta, three to seven servings of protein or dairy, three to five servings of fat and no more than 75 calories of sugar a day.

In general, you can eat healthy by eating more fruits, vegetables and whole grains. Reduce your intake of saturated fat, trans fat and cholesterol. Limit sweets and salt. Drink alcoholic beverages in moderation. Control portion sizes and the total number of calories you consume.

Exercise is the other important component of a healthy lifestyle. It's best if you can exercise for at least 30 minutes five times a week. Fitness experts suggest that, of the 30 minutes, 20 should be spent in some form of cardio exercise, five in stretching and five in resistance training.

I find that it's best to choose a time to exercise and build your daily schedule around it. Some people like first thing in the morning. Others like the evening. I prefer midday. I find that if I exercise around noon, I am less hungry and consume fewer calories at lunch.

Hydration and circulation are important, too. Drink plenty of water. It keeps you hydrated and helps combat hunger. If you spent a lot of time at your desk, take a few minutes every hour to get up and stretch. You can do leg lifts and stomach squeezes at your desk. A little bit of activity can give you a burst of oxygen that will energize you and keep you feeling good.

You don't have to become a fitness fanatic to be a high performer. Eating well and exercising, however, will keep you sharp and on top of your game. It will keep your stress in check. And while a little stress is a good thing, too much can knock you out of the game.

Section 5

Create Positive Personal Impact

A ll successful people create positive personal impact. Positive personal impact is like charisma, only more so. People gravitate towards people with positive personal impact. When you create positive personal impact, other people want to be around you. They want to work with you. They want to be your friend and colleague.

People with positive personal impact develop and nurture their personal brand. They are impeccable in their presentation of self. They know and follow the basic rules of etiquette. If you master these three keys, you'll create positive personal impact.

I have a model of customer service that I use with my consulting clients. It begins with the premise that after any interaction, your customers R.A.T.E. you. The people in your life R.A.T.E. you, too. You can use your R.A.T.E.ing to build positive personal impact. It works like this…

R stands for Responsiveness;
A stands for Assurance;
T stands for Tangibles;
E stands for Empathy.

If you notice, only one of the four points in the model – tangibles – is what you actually do for, or deliver to, the people in your life. The other three are the emotional measures people judge you by. These are as important as the tangibles, especially when it comes to creating positive personal impact.

You have to deliver the tangibles. You must produce results. That's the cost of a ticket to the corporate career success sweepstakes.

You have to pay attention to the other three factors – responsiveness, assurance and empathy – to make a positive personal impact while you're performing. Let's look at each in detail.

Responsiveness. You have to ensure that the people in your life see you as someone who is willing to help, someone who understands what needs to be done and is willing to do it. Other people need to think that you will give them what they want, when they want it and in a manner that they can use it.

Assurance. You have to be able to convey trust and confidence. People need to feel that you are going to deliver. To do this, you must be knowledgeable about the people in your life and their needs and wants. You need to be clear on what you can offer to help them meet their goals. You need to ensure that they are confident that you will do what you say you will do.

Empathy. The people in your life must perceive you as an individual who understands, cares about and pays attention to their needs. To do this, you need to be willing to walk a mile in other people's shoes. You have to demonstrate to them that you're aware of and are sensitive to their unique and individual needs.

Debra Benton is a friend of mine. She is also a very good executive coach. Debra has a way of dispensing great common sense advice in an easy to remember and easy to use manner. Her book *Executive Charisma* is no exception.

In the last chapter, Debra urges readers not to do what they would "typically do." "Embrace the opposite, or at least a variation of the opposite." Her advice is somewhat counter-intuitive until you look at it closely.

Here are some of the opposites Debra suggests:

"Go against the social norm without being weird or stupid. It's impossible to do something spectacular unless you do the opposite from the majority.

Initiate when others won't.

Expect acceptance instead of feeling undeserved or unequal to others.

Give acceptance instead of judging.

Ask favors instead of do, do, do.

Stand tall, even when you're too tired.

Smile when you don't feel like it.

Show humanness versus reverting to your role.

Use humor when things are serious.

Touch when you are afraid.

Slow down when you have a lot to do.

Shut up when you have a lot to say.

Listen when you don't want to."

Debra goes on to say...

"Doing the opposite isn't being stubborn, or obstinate. It's being flexible, adaptable, open-minded, willing to avoid the obvious and do the unexpected... and brave in doing something differently from the way you did it before."

That's some common sense.

I particularly like Debra's idea, "Listen when you don't want to." Most of us, myself included, tend to tune out people we don't like, or who begin a conversation by saying something we disagree with. These are the times to listen the hardest because they're the best opportunity to learn something new or to reframe a problem.

Successful people create positive personal impact. You can create positive personal impact by doing the opposite of what people expect you to do. Follow Debra Benton's advice. "Shut up when you have a lot to say." "Listen when you don't want to." "Give acceptance instead of judging." When you do these things, you'll be building a personal brand that defines you as someone whom others want to work with.

Chapter 16

Be of
Strong Character

I'm a Penn State alum. Joe Paterno, our football coach is a living legend. He's 84 and still coaching. He's won more games than any other Division I coach. He also donated several million dollars to the university to help expand the library. Joe is an interesting guy.

I was watching a Penn State game on television last fall. The announcer said something that sums up the way Joe has run the football program at Penn State for the past 45 years....

"I want my players to be physically fit. I want them to be mentally fit. And I want them to be morally fit."

Morally fit is another way of saying "Be of strong character."

I wrote those words before the child sex abuse scandal that engulfed the Penn State football program and Joe Paterno's death. Joe had information that a retired Penn State coach and personal friend was probably sexually abusing young boys. He reported this to his boss, the athletic director, but not to the police.

Joe did what was required of him – report allegations of sexual impropriety to his boss. But he didn't do the moral thing. He didn't take steps to make sure that this alleged conduct by a friend would stop. In other words, he wasn't morally fit – and this is very sad for me and the Penn State family.

Joe Paterno's case demonstrates the importance of being of strong character. This one lapse – albeit a big one – has cost him his legacy. That's sad for Joe but it's sadder for the children who were allegedly abused by Jerry Sandusky.

Martin Seligman of the University of Pennsylvania and Christopher Peterson of the University of Michigan have written a book that helps define what it means to be of strong character. *Character Strengths and Virtues: A Handbook and Classification* identifies 24 character traits, grouped into six strengths. I found this book to be a kind of 21st century I Ching.

I spent $55 to download it to my Kindle and read all 800 pages. Here is a summary of the six strengths and 24 character traits.

Strengths of Wisdom and Knowledge: Cognitive strengths that entail the acquisition and use of knowledge.

1. *Creativity [originality, ingenuity]*: Thinking of novel and productive ways to conceptualize and do things.

2. *Curiosity [interest, novelty-seeking, being open to experience]*: Taking an interest in ongoing experience for its own sake; exploring and discovering.

3. *Open-mindedness [judgment, critical thinking]*: Thinking things through and examining them from all sides; weighing all evidence fairly.

4. *Love of learning*: Mastering new skills, topics, and bodies of knowledge, whether on one's own or formally.

5. *Perspective [wisdom]*: Being able to provide wise counsel to others; having ways of looking at the world that make sense to oneself and to other people.

Strengths of Courage: Emotional strengths that involve the exercise of will to accomplish goals in the face of opposition, external and internal.

6. *Bravery [valor]*: Not shrinking from threat, challenge, difficulty, or pain; acting on convictions even if unpopular.

7. *Persistence [perseverance, industriousness]*: Finishing what one starts; persisting in a course of action in spite of obstacles.

8. *Integrity [authenticity, honesty]*: Presenting oneself in a genuine way; taking responsibility for one's feeling and actions.

9. *Vitality [zest, enthusiasm, vigor, energy]*: Approaching life with excitement and energy; feeling alive and activated.

Strengths of Humanity: Interpersonal strengths that involve tending and befriending others.

10. *Love*: Valuing close relations with others, in particular those in which sharing and caring are reciprocated.

11. *Kindness [generosity, nurturance, care, compassion, altruistic love, "niceness"]*: Doing favors and good deeds for others.

12. *Social intelligence [emotional intelligence, personal intelligence]*: Being aware of the motives and feelings of other people and oneself.

Strengths of Justice: Civic strengths that underlie healthy community life.

13. *Citizenship [social responsibility, loyalty, teamwork]*: Working well as a member of a group or team; being loyal to the group.

14. *Fairness*: Treating all people the same according to notions of fairness and justice; not letting personal feelings bias decisions about others.

15. *Leadership*: Encouraging a group of which one is a member, to get things done and at the same maintain time good relations within the group.

Strengths of Temperance: Strengths that protect against excess.

16. *Forgiveness and mercy*: Forgiving those who have done wrong; accepting the shortcomings of others; giving people a second chance; not being vengeful.

17. *Humility / Modesty*: Letting one's accomplishments speak for themselves; not regarding oneself as more special than one is.
18. *Prudence*: Being careful about one's choices; not taking undue risks; not saying or doing things that might later be regretted.
19. *Self-regulation [self-control]*: Regulating what one feels and does; being disciplined; controlling one's appetites and emotions.

Strengths of Transcendence: Strengths that forge connections to the larger universe and provide meaning.

20. *Appreciation of beauty and excellence [awe, wonder, elevation]*: Appreciating beauty, excellence, and/or skilled performance in various domains of life.
21. *Gratitude*: Being aware of and thankful for the good things that happen; taking time to express thanks.
22. *Hope [optimism, future-mindedness, future orientation]*: Expecting the best in the future and working to achieve it.
23. *Humor [playfulness]*: Liking to laugh and tease; bringing smiles to other people; seeing the light side.
24. *Spirituality [religiousness, faith, purpose]*: Having coherent beliefs about the higher purpose, the meaning of life, and the meaning of the universe.

I read an article in the *New York Times Magazine* about this book. It said in part...

> "In most societies these strengths are considered to have a moral valence. In many cases they overlap with religious laws and strictures. But their true importance did not come from their relationships to any system of ethics or moral laws but from their practical benefit: cultivating these strengths represented a reliable path to 'the good life,' a life that was not just happy, but also meaningful and fulfilling."

These six strengths and 24 character traits are a common sense roadmap for building character and creating your corporate career success.

Here is what I suggest you do to wrap your head around them...

Take out a sheet of paper. Create three columns. List the character traits in the left column. Label the center column "A real strength for me;" label the third column, "I need to work on this." Then think about each character trait and put an X in column that most describes you. This takes courage but I guarantee that it will be a valuable exercise if you're serious about creating the life and career success you want and deserve.

I did this exercise and decided that I need to work on seven of the character traits...

- Creativity
- Bravery
- Persistence

- Love
- Forgiveness and Mercy
- Prudence
- Self-Regulation

Three of the seven – Forgiveness and Mercy, Prudence and Self-Regulation – fall into the Temperance strength, and two of the seven – Bravery and Persistence – fall into the Courage strength.

Here's my honest self-evaluation on the area in which I need to improve...

Forgiveness and Mercy is defined as, "Forgiving those who have done wrong; accepting the shortcomings of others; giving people a second chance; not being vengeful." I am not a vengeful person but there are times when it's difficult for me to forgive and forget. I need to be less judgmental and do a better job of letting bygones be bygones. I do give people second chances but I have a hard time forgetting real or perceived wrongs I've experienced.

Prudence is defined as, "Being careful about one's choices; not taking undue risks; not saying or doing things that might later be regretted." I sometimes act impulsively. I have a tendency to make decisions without weighing the pros and cons. I have got better at this as I've got older but it's still an area I need to work on. When I was younger, I said and did things that got me in trouble. I am better at that now. I think before I speak more often and hold my counsel when appropriate.

Self-Regulation is defined as, "Regulating what one feels and does; being disciplined; controlling one's appetites and emotions." All my life, I have struggled with weight. I work at being disciplined about what I eat and how much I exercise. Still, I often eat more than I need and I often eat things that aren't healthy. I'm better at this than I once was but it's still a constant battle. I have got better at exercising. I am more disciplined about it. I like to bike. It's good exercise but there are days when I choose to not do it. On the other hand, I was able to cut alcohol out of my life. I haven't had a drink in more than 20 years. I was a beer drinker – and beer is nothing but empty calories. Not drinking helps my weight and helps with Prudence. I am less likely to do and say inappropriate things when I am not drinking.

Bravery is defined as, "Not shrinking from threat, challenge, difficulty, or pain; acting on convictions even if unpopular." I am physically brave. One of my rugby mates once described me as "someone who never took a backward step on the pitch." I often don't act, however, on my convictions. I detest racism, sexism and homophobia. Yet, sometimes I am silent in the company of racists, sexists and homophobes. To me, this is a lack of moral bravery. I need to be more willing to confront racism, sexism and homophobia when I encounter them before I can truly call myself a brave person.

Persistence is defined as, "Finishing what one starts; persisting in a course of action in spite of obstacles." I see this one as pass/fail. I'm pretty persistent. It takes a lot to knock me off course once I start something. For example, I'm committed to blogging. I've written five blog posts a week, 50 weeks a year for seven years. That takes persistence. Still, there are projects I've begun and not finished. Writing a novel is one. I've started it at least 10 times and have never finished. Until I finish every project I start, I won't give myself a positive rating on persistence.

Creativity is defined as "Thinking of novel and productive ways to conceptualize and do things." I tend to think of myself as creative. When confronted with something truly novel, however, I realize that I often go with the tried and true. I attribute this more to expediency than to lack of creativity. Before I can say that I am truly creative, I need to begin looking at everything I do with fresh, unbiased eyes.

Love is defined as "Valuing close relations with others, in particular those in which sharing and caring are reciprocated." I can be self-absorbed. I can let my work interfere with my relationship with my wife. I get lost in books, spending hours reading when my relationships would be better served by engaging in conversation. I am not an unthoughtful person. I do need, however, to be more in tune with the needs of those who love me.

That's my assessment of myself on the Seligman and Peterson character traits. This wasn't an easy exercise for me. I doubt it will be easy for you. But I urge you to do give it a go. Be honest with yourself. You'll find things you like and things you don't. But identifying your character flaws is the first step in becoming a person of high character.

Chapter 17

Build Your Personal Brand

When you think of great brands, what products come to mind? Coca- Cola, Levi's jeans, *The New York Times,* Apple computers and Scotch Tape are a few that come to my mind when I hear "brand." People can be brands, too: LeBron James, Oprah Winfrey, Martha Stewart. In fact, they're recognizable by their first names. Tiger Woods was once the best-known personal brand. His personal problems ruined that.

If you want to become a corporate career success, you need to brand yourself. Your personal brand differentiates you from everyone else in the world. My brand is "The Common Sense Guy." Because of my brand, people know that they can rely on me for common sense advice that can help them reach their career, life and business goals. They also know that they will get this advice in a straightforward, easy to understand and apply manner, because, after all, I'm just a guy.

Spend time crafting your brand. Think of it this way. Your brand is the two or three words you want people to most often associate with you. Decide what you want these words to be and then go about making sure that all of the people with whom you come into contact think of you that way.

This is important because nature abhors a vacuum. If you don't brand yourself, others will. It's better to be in control of your personal brand by creating it yourself than it is to let others create it for you.

Here's a real-life example. I have a very successful friend. He owns a high-profile and growing advertising agency. We met when we were both working for a Fortune 500 company. My friend is a fun guy, a big sports fan and very witty. Somehow, his fun personality got him tagged as "immature." This is ironic because he is one of the most mature and hard-working people I know. No matter, his immature brand cost him several promotions. He finally had to leave the company and begin someplace anew where he could establish a more positive brand.

Creating a strong personal brand is simple conceptually. Just answer these questions: "How do I want people to think of me?" "What words do I want people to use to describe me?" Think about these questions. Take your time. Answer them. Then do whatever it takes to make sure that other people think of you that way.

For example, if you decide that "hard-working" is a term you would like others to associate with you, then work hard. Do your assignments well and on time. When you finish one task, ask for another. Come early, stay late. Ask questions to help you understand the business. Pretty soon, people will begin thinking of you as a hard worker – "someone who does everything we ask, and then asks for more." Once this happens, you'll know that you're on your way to creating your own special and unique personal brand.

You're smart enough to figure out what to do to create the brand you want. The important thing is to choose your brand, then consistently and constantly do the things that build the brand that is uniquely yours.

A unique and distinctive personal brand is a big part of creating positive personal impact. Your brand should reflect your uniqueness. There is one thing, however, that I believe should be a part of everyone's personal brand – integrity.

According to Wikipedia, "Integrity is consistency of actions, values, methods, measures and principles." Integrity and consistency are intertwined. People who are consistent in their actions are seen as people with a high degree of integrity.

I once saw a quote from Oprah Winfrey: "Real integrity is doing the right thing, knowing that nobody's going to know whether you did it or not." This is true. If you practice situational ethics – doing the right thing only when you're in the public eye – you aren't really a person of high integrity, you're just pretending to be one.

Besides, it's hard to act one way in public and another in private. So to be safe, resolve to act like Oprah. Do the right thing because it's the right thing to do – not because you'll get creditor avoid getting into trouble.

John Maxwell is a well-known business author. One of his

books sends the same message. It's called *There's No Such Thing As Business Ethics: There's Only One Rule for Making Decisions.* According to John, that rule is the Golden Rule: "Do unto others as you would have them do unto you." In other words, do the right thing.

There's a practical side to this, too. Mark Twain once said, "If you tell the truth, you don't have to remember anything." In other words, if you're always a person of high integrity, it's easy to be a person of high integrity. There are no complicating factors – like remembering what you did or said in a given situation.

Speaking through Polonius, Shakespeare gives similar advice in *Hamlet.* "To thine own self be true, and it must follow as the day the night, thou canst be false to no man." Roy Blackman, my father-in-law, passed away a few years ago. This quote was his epitaph. It was on the program handed out at his funeral. Roy embodied it in how he lived his life. It was the only piece of advice he gave his grandson, Matt, as he went off to college.

Oprah, John Maxwell, Mark Twain and Shakespeare all agree on one common sense point. If you want to become known as a person of high integrity – and I believe integrity is the cornerstone of any personal brand – act as a person of high integrity all the time – not just when it suits you or when someone might notice.

Here's a story to illustrate this point. My wife Cathy was a flight attendant for 36 years. Seniority is a very important thing in the airline industry. It governs how you bid for trips, positions on the airplane and vacations – almost anything important to a flight attendant's quality of work life.

Cathy was active in her union. And seniority was one of the union's most sacred principles. A few years before she retired, her airline made a big push into the international market. International flights were plum assignments and went to those with high seniority. The airline realized, however, that it would be to their advantage to have some flight attendants who spoke the language of the country to which they were flying. Most flight attendants spoke only English. The airline proposed putting two "language speakers" on each international flight. Many people, including Cathy, were upset with this arrangement, as they felt it violated the seniority concept.

Cathy used to fly from the U.S. to London. One day, I said to her, "This whole language speaker issue doesn't really affect you. You fly to London. There are no language speakers on those flights. Why do you care so much?" She said, "I believe in the concept of seniority. It doesn't matter if I'm affected by language speakers. It's the principal of the thing." That's consistency – and integrity in action.

Chapter 18

Be Impeccable in Your Presentation of Self

Your appearance says a lot about you. My advice in this area to create positive personal impact is simple: Dress one level up. In other words, dress a little nicer than you have to. For example, if your office is casual, wear a dress or a suit every once in a while.

Make sure your clothes and shoes are clean and in good repair. Keep your hair clean and well styled. Make sure your shoes are shined. Look in the mirror on your way out the door. Ask yourself, "Will I impress other people with the way I look today?" If the answer is "no," take a few minutes and change before you go to work.

I always get dressed up when I am meeting clients. Many of my clients dress casually. When they tell me, "You didn't need to wear a suit today," I say, "Yes, I did. I'm meeting with an important person – you." Show respect for yourself and the people around you by dressing well and looking good.

Accessories are another part of your appearance. In general, you want your accessories to complement, not overpower, your clothing. Keep them understated and elegant. Large rings and earrings or bracelets that jangle when you move can distract from your professionalism. Save the bling for evenings out. At work, tone it down.

Pay attention to your electronic accessories, too. About a year ago, I saw a *Wall Street Journal* article about electronic accessories. It made some interesting points about cell phones, PDAs and other electronic helpers – all small enough for you to tote around – and how they can hurt your image as a professional. Look around, you'll see that most senior executives aren't over-burdened by electronic accessories.

In *Wildly Sophisticated*, my friend Nicole Williams lays out 10 fashion commandments. I think they are invaluable for creating a professional look…

1. **Sweat the small stuff.**

   People don't necessarily notice if you're groomed but they definitely notice when you're not.

2. **Restrain yourself.**

   Never let your accessories wear you.

3. **Know your body.**

   Recognize that every style trend is not designed for you. This isn't a limitation – it's just reality.

4. **Black is your friend.**

   Black staples – pants, skirts and jackets – are clean, classic and always look good. They're flattering, will work with everything else in your closet and will stretch your clothing budget.

5. **Focus on your feet.**

   A great pair of shoes can make all the difference in your look. Make sure your footwear is polished and clean. This is another one of those details that people really do notice.

6. **Welcome the three-way mirror.**

   Clothes that fit well make you look better and help your confidence.

7. **Work it.**

   Style is really a synonym for self-expression. You'll feel and look better when your clothes reflect your personality.

8. **Buy quality.**

   In the long run, quality clothes will actually save you money.

9. **Invest in accessories.**

   Your bag or briefcase is a constant companion. Clients, employers and colleagues will notice what's draped on your arm. Invest in a quality piece that reflects your style. And in this age of laptops, cell phones and PDAs, a bag that will carry your hardware is a lifesaver.

10. Relax.

Bottom line? It's just fashion. Give it your best shot. Know that style matters and that looking groomed and professional are important for your career.

Your online presence counts, too. Recently, I heard a startling claim: 45% of employers use search engines and social networking sites to research job candidates. I was startled because the number was so low. I would have expected it to be closer to 90%.

Your web presence can enhance or detract from your image. Successful people use the web to enhance their brand and image. The first step is to see what's already out there about you on the web. Review at least the first five pages of results from search engines including Google, Yahoo and MSN. Clean up your web image. Remove anything on MySpace or Facebook you wouldn't want your mother – or an employer or customer – to see.

If you think that people don't Google you, think again. People do use search engines to learn about you before they meet you. Here's just one example. Before she retired, Sylvia Montero was the Executive VP of HR for Pfizer Inc. She is a friend of mine. I have mentioned her in my blog posts. She once told me that a woman who was booking her to speak at a conference said that she had Googled her and that my blog posts were among the first things to come up.

With ever smaller cameras and recording devices, this situation has taken a different turn. Now you have to pay attention to what others post about you online. I read an op-ed piece by a Harvard student who said that these days you have to be careful what you do at parties. He said that students worry about whether their friends post pictures of them taken at parties. Apparently, it's not uncommon for students with cell phone cameras to take photos of their friends who are making out or drinking from a keg and shout "blackmail photo." Our public and private lives are becoming less distinct. A lot of what can get posted on the web about you is not in your control, so pay attention.

This doesn't mean you should have no fun. It does mean that you need to pay close attention to your behavior at all times. In some ways, that's too bad. I know I wouldn't want to have many of my college, or young adult, exploits posted on the web. Good thing for me that we didn't have cell phone cameras and web cams in those days.

While technology can hinder your efforts to present yourself positively and professionally, it also can help. Many people have a variety of online accounts. I'm an old guy and I have accounts at LinkedIn, Facebook, MySpace, Plaxo, Yahoo 360, Success Television, Jason's Network and Duct Tape Marketing Workbench. I write a blog. I Twitter.

You not only need to dress for success, you need to have a simple, easy-to-find, clean web presence. Give your online presence as much attention as you do your personal appearance.

Even if you're not in business for yourself, you need to have a web presence to create positive personal impact. These days, I often hear, "If you don't exist online, do you really exist?" That's a good question. Prospective employers and customers will Google you.

You'll be better off if they like what they see. It's much better than if they find unfavorable results or nothing at all. Today, when people want to learn about you, they get most of their answers from Google.

This can be pretty scary – if you don't take the time to make sure that you have an Internet presence that reflects well on you. The best place to begin is with your unique personal brand. Your personal brand highlights what is special and unique about you – why you are not a commodity.

For my money, the best book on personal branding is *Career Distinction* by William Arruda and Kirsten Dixson. They stress the importance of the "Three C's" – Clarity, Consistency and Constancy. You can use the Internet to help you with all three C's.

I'm a big believer in social networking sites to help you build your brand online. LinkedIn, Facebook, MySpace and Twitter are great places to build relationships with like-minded people. Choose the social network where you have the greatest affinity with the people on it. For my money, LinkedIn is the best social network for corporate career success.

Leaving comments on targeted blogs is another good way to build your brand online. This means that you read blogs that are tied to your field or area of expertise and comment on posts that interest you. I used to be bad about this. I read quite a few blogs but commented infrequently. I set a goal to leave at least five comments on blogs per day. That's 25 comments a week. I've stuck to it and it has paid off. I have raised my web presence by commenting on other people's blogs.

Of course, I am in business for myself and my web presence is very important to me. You don't have to do 25 comments a week. Start small. One comment a day is a reasonable goal if you have limited time.

Starting your own blog and posting two or three times a week is another good way to build your online presence and enhance your personal brand. This assumes, of course, that you have something to say. And, in my opinion, everyone has something to say.

Online book reviews are another way to build your brand. Do you read a lot? If so, take a few minutes and review books that you like on Amazon.com. Because I blog about books quite a bit, I have started to receive complimentary review copies from major publishing houses – a real bonus and money saver.

A while back, I decided to post only positive reviews. If I don't like a book, I don't do a negative review. I do this because there are enough interesting, well-written books out there. I choose to focus on them, instead of bashing those books (however few) I don't like. This way, I am building a web presence as a kind and helpful guy.

The common sense point here is simple. Use the Internet to build your personal brand by paying attention to your Internet presence. Focus on the "three C's" – Clarity, Consistency, and Constancy – when building your brand online.

In my opinion, LinkedIn is the best social networking site for building your career success. It is frequented by professionals – people just like you. There are more than 35 million professionals on LinkedIn. Chris Muccio, David Burns and Peggy Murrah have written a great 42 Rules book called *42 Rules for 24-Hour Success on LinkedIn*. It is my bible for brand building via LinkedIn. LinkedIn is the best social networking site for professionals. It is a place to find people and for people to find you. It gives you a communication tool to create a platform for your success.

In *42 Rules for 24-Hour Success on LinkedIn*, Chris, David and Peggy show you how to use LinkedIn to do the simple things to achieve success 24 hours a day. Remember, the Internet never sleeps.

Your LinkedIn profile is the place to begin. It can help you build your brand. A good profile will attract others, educate them about you and influence their feelings towards you – even if you've never met in person. Chris, David and Peggy say that you have three seconds to communicate your brand on your LinkedIn profile. Make those seconds count.

The LinkedIn site lets you create a "professional description." Before reading *42 Rules for 24-Hour Success on LinkedIn*, and speaking with Chris and Peggy, my professional description read "Bud Bilanich, The Common Sense Guy." Now it reads, "Bud Bilanich: I help individuals, teams and entire organizations succeed by helping them apply their common sense." I don't know about you, but I think that the second professional description is much stronger, communicates better and makes the most out of my three seconds.

You can leverage your LinkedIn profile in several ways. Invite everyone you know to connect with you on LinkedIn. Use the LinkedIn colleagues and classmates reconnect function. It can be a lot of fun to reconnect with people you used to know. If you use Microsoft Outlook, download the Outlook toolbar. It will let you know the LinkedIn status of everyone you receive email from. Ask your existing LinkedIn connections to introduce you to their connections. This way, you can build a network of people exposed to your brand.

Chris, David and Peggy showed me how the LinkedIn "What you are working on now" function can help build your brand. Update it regularly. Post the interesting things you are doing – at work and in your life. This will help others get to know you better and will showcase the depth and breadth of your experience. Think of it as a longer Tweet. Twitter limits you to 140 characters per post. Here you can post three or four sentences and go into a little more detail.

And, just like Twitter, people can respond to your LinkedIn "What you are working on now" posts. This creates the opportunity to engage in dialogue with those you meet on LinkedIn, strengthening your relationships.

LinkedIn Groups are another powerful way to leverage the power of LinkedIn. You can find groups by seeing which groups people with interests similar to yours join. You can use the LinkedIn search tool for this. Chris, David and Peggy suggest joining no more than three groups at first. Spend some time in these groups. See if they appeal to you. If they do, become active by participating in conversations, sharing your thoughts and ideas and links you find helpful. If you don't like a group, drop out and find another.

Groups can be time-consuming. Chris, David and Peggy suggest setting your default to receive emails from groups once a week. Then set aside a period each week to read and reply to posts.

LinkedIn is a great social networking tool – if you leverage it correctly. *42 Rules for 24-Hour Success on LinkedIn* is a great guide to using LinkedIn for building your brand and web presence.

Chapter 19

Know and Follow the Basic Rules of Business Etiquette

A ll that stuff your mother told you about being polite is true. You can't go wrong acting like a lady or gentleman. I try to be a gentleman at all times.

My friend Sharon Hill, author of *The Wild Woman's Guide to Etiquette,* makes a great point about the difference between manners and etiquette. Manners are about kindness and caring about others. Etiquette is protocol, rules of behavior you need to learn and use. Manners come from your heart, etiquette comes from your head. Ladies and gentlemen are both well-mannered and observe the rules of etiquette.

If you follow the rules of etiquette, you won't look foolish in social situations. You will be admired for demonstrating class and confidence. Proper etiquette can help you get ahead in business because you'll create a positive impression. Sometimes, you won't even know that people are watching, but believe me, someone usually is.

Manners, on the other hand, distinguish you as a caring person, someone who values every human being. Well-mannered people treat others with kindness that reinforces their self-worth. You can know and follow all the rules and still not be well-mannered. While it's important to follow the rules, if I had to choose between manners and etiquette, manners would win every time.

Handwritten thank-you notes are a great way to distinguish yourself as a lady or gentleman. They show both good manners and proper etiquette. Here are three tips for writing thank- you notes: 1) Write legibly. 2) Always identify the gift you received – be specific. Your note will be more personal this way. 3) Always mention how you plan on using the gift. You can create all sorts of positive personal impact with thank-you notes.

These days, there are companies who will do what I call "faux handwritten notes." They take a sample of your handwriting and then use it to create messages that they send on your behalf. In my opinion, these cards are better than an email but they still don't substitute for a handwritten note. Two reasons: First, you still have to compose the message and email it to the vendor; and second, while these cards look pretty good, they still don't have the personal touch of a note written by hand.

As with most things, there is one rule of etiquette that I always follow. I always do whatever I can to help the people around me feel comfortable. Ladies and gentlemen make sure that others are comfortable.

For example, when you are dining out with others, you may know that your water glass is on the right and that your bread and butter plate is on the left. Other people may not know this. So if someone uses your bread plate, don't say "Hey, that's mine – yours is over there." Just place your roll on your dinner plate. Being right is no excuse for embarrassing someone else.

Remember, friends can help take you where you want to go. Etiquette and manners will help you make those friends.

Learn and use proper dining etiquette. Business meals are either a great opportunity to make a positive personal impact. Or they can be disasters waiting to happen. If you follow the simple rules of dining etiquette, you'll be fine.

Here is advice on making the best of the opportunity business meals afford you. First, use common sense. These rules aren't all that complicated and your common sense will tell you what to do.

Learn basic table manners and etiquette. Place settings can be a bit of a challenge, especially when there are a lot of people crammed around a small, round table. If you remember that your water glass is to your right and your bread and butter plate is to your left, you'll be off to a good start. If someone uses your bread plate, don't say anything. Use your main plate for your bread. You won't inconvenience the person to your right or embarrass the person to your left.

Your salad fork is the little one on the far left and your soup spoon is the big one on the far right. If you remember this and work from the outside in, you'll be unlikely to make any cutlery mistakes. Sharon Hill has come up with a clever way of remembering where things are on a table: BMW. Moving from left to right, you will find your bread plate (B), then your meal plate (M) and finally your water (or anything wet) (W).

There are a few simple courtesies that can help you get through any business meal. Place your napkin in your lap as soon as you sit down. Sit up straight. Keep your elbows off the table. You can rest your wrists on the table.

Cocktails and beer are before dinner. Wine accompanies dinner. Drink alcohol in moderation.

If you choose not to drink wine with your meal, do not turn over your wine glass. Simply say "no thanks" when the waiter is pouring for the table.

Wait until everyone at the table has been served before you begin to eat. If one person's food is delayed and he or she suggests that you should begin eating, feel free to do so. Order things that are easy to eat.

Order with care. It's almost impossible to eat pasta that needs to be twirled and look sophisticated doing it. Order foods that are easy to eat. Lobster, snails, shrimp with the tails on are good things to avoid when you are business dining.

Break – don't cut – bread or rolls. That's why dining is called "breaking bread." Pass the salt and pepper shaker as a pair – even if someone asks for only one. Spoon soup away from you. This will help you avoid spilling it on yourself. Sip soup don't slurp it.

When you are finished eating, place your knife and fork on your plate at 4 o'clock. Fold your napkin and place it to the left of your plate. This will indicate to the server that you are finished with your meal.

These are simple rules that should help you get through business meals with grace and aplomb. One final thing to remember is that business meals are not about the food. I have a personal story about this. Read on.

Business meals are about business not the food. Remember this the next time you are invited to share a meal – whether breakfast, lunch or dinner – with a business colleague. As I've mentioned, knowing dining etiquette rules is a good place to start. It's also important to pay attention to what you order.

Here's a personal story that really makes this point.

About 30 years ago, I had just accepted a job as the training manager for a division of a large company. Our division was in New Haven, Connecticut, a city with a large Italian population and a lot of great Italian restaurants.

About a month after I began my job, the VP of Human Resources was hosting a two-day meeting of all of the senior HR people in the company at our division. Junior people like me were invited to a dinner after the first day of the meeting. I was looking forward to this as an opportunity to impress senior people in other divisions.

One of my junior colleagues was a local woman. She was excited about the choice of the restaurant. Of course, it was an Italian restaurant. She had been there on special occasions with her husband. She was very fond of a dish called *zuppa de pesce,* a medley of seafood served over spaghetti. A couple of days before the meeting, she told me about that this dish. She added that it was available for two only and asked if I would be willing to share it with her. I said, "Sure."

We arrived at the restaurant, and sure enough, *zuppa di pesce* was on the menu. My friend and I ordered it. What a disaster!

First, the waiter brought lobster bibs for us. No one else had ordered the dish, so we were the only ones with bibs. When the food arrived, everyone had a dish of pasta, grilled fish or a steak. The *zuppa di pesce* was served on a silver tray so big the waiter had to bring a side table. There was enough fish and pasta to feed the entire table. My friend dug in and really enjoyed it. I felt like a character in the movie *The Godfather*.

I tried to carry on an intelligent conversation with people I wanted to impress while wearing a lobster bib and trying hard to not spill sauce on my suit.

I didn't lose any points that night but I didn't make any either. It was apparent to others that I was there for the food not for the conversation.

I learned a lesson that day. Always order something that won't call attention to you when you eat it. I try to be a good friend and in social situations, I'll often share an entrée for two only. I won't, however, do it at business dinners or lunches because they aren't about food. They're about the conversation.

Section 6

Become a Dynamic Communicator

A t first glance, the life of a business traveler, especially one like me who travels to New York City regularly, appears glamorous. People always ask if I've eaten at famous restaurants like "21" or the latest hot spot they've read about in *Travel and Leisure.*

When I'm in New York and don't have a business dinner scheduled, I usually dine on Chinese take-out in my hotel room. My fortune cookie once read, "Your talents will be recognized and suitably rewarded." I was happy with this but it made me think.

My talents, your talents, everyone's talents, will be recognized and rewarded if we develop and use our communication skills. There are three types of communication skills critically important for career and life success: 1) conversation skills; 2) writing skills; and 3) presentation skills.

You need to develop each of them if you want to have your talents recognized.

There are a few common sense points associated with becoming a dynamic communicator.

You become a good conversationalist by listening. Take an active interest in other people and what they're saying. Show them you're listening by asking follow-up questions to what they say.

Conversation skills enhance your networking ability. Networking is an important but often overlooked communication skill. It is helpful when you are looking for a job. It's even more important when you're happy with your situation. All people who are professionally successful build and nurture strong networks.

Networking is an important skill. Successful people have large networks. They have people they can call to help them. They know they can call on these people because these people know they can call on them. That's the real secret of networking – looking to help others, not just to finding out how they can help you.

Write in a way that communicates well. In general, this means being clear, concise and easily readable. The best way to make sure your writing is readable is to read it aloud before sending it.

When I was in high school, I was the editor of my yearbook. To raise funds to cover the cost of the yearbook, we sold ads. There were a lot of factories in the town where I grew up. Past yearbook staffs had never approached these factories to place ads in the yearbook. I wrote sales letters to all the plant managers. The result was several full-page ads.

One plant manager wrote back, asking if I would come see him. When I introduced myself in his office, he was surprised. He said that my sales letter was so well-written that he thought I was the teacher who was the yearbook sponsor. Two years later, I was looking for a summer job after my first year of college. The market was tight. I called this man. He remembered me and I got a job.

Preparation is the most important key to good presentations. To be a great presenter, you have to analyze your audience, prepare a talk that gives them what they want and practice your talk out loud.

Presentation skills may be the biggest opportunity for getting your talents noticed. Just a few months ago, I did a talk for a

Chamber of Commerce. As it so happens, the sheriff's department is a member of this Chamber. The sheriff himself happened to be there that day. He liked my talk. About a week later, I got a call from his training office. The sheriff asked them to get in touch with me to do supervisory training for the department's sergeants. I never would have got this business if it weren't for the notice I received from a talk at that Chamber meeting.

The Dilbert cartoon strip often focuses on poor communication. I cut out the ones I really like. Here's one from a Sunday paper...

> Dilbert approaches his boss (you know, the one with the tufts of hair that look like devil's horns) and says, "The security audit accidentally locked all developers out of the system." The boss says, "Well, it is what it is."
>
> Dilbert says, "How does that help?" The boss replies, "You don't know what you don't know." Dilbert, obviously frustrated, says, "Congratulations, you're the first human to fail the Turing test." The boss says, "What does that mean?" Dilbert replies, "It is what it is," to which the boss says, "Why didn't you say so in the first place?"

There really is such a thing as a Turing test. Dictionary.com defines it as follows: "A test proposed by British mathematician Alan Turing, and often used as a test of whether a computer has humanlike intelligence. If a panel of human beings conversing with an unknown entity (via keyboard, for example) believes that that entity is human, and if the entity is actually a computer, then the computer is said to have passed the Turing test."

This is pretty funny. It is also kind of sad since it's indicative of the lack of communication in today's business world. Scott Adams, Dilbert's creator, really gets it when it comes to workplace communication problems.

*Beyond Bullsh*t*, by UCLA Anderson School of Management Professor Samuel Culbert, is an interesting little book. Culbert defines bullsh*t in the following way…

> "It is telling people what you think they need to hear. It may involve finessing the truth or outright lying, but the purpose is always self-serving. And while I appreciate the role of some b.s. in keeping the corporate peace, it makes people feel beaten up, deceived – even dirty. When people talk straight at work, companies make out better because the best idea usually wins. In contrast, when people are bullsh*tting, they hide their mistakes and the company suffers. Straight talk is the product of relationships built on trust."

Phrases like "it is what it is" are not straight talk. They are part of the inexplicable jargon that has overtaken us. Dynamic communicators say what they mean in an easily understood manner. Effective communicators don't show off their large vocabularies. Instead, they choose words that are the most easily understood and get their point across.

Dynamic communicators eschew, I mean, don't use, jargon.

They avoid meaningless phrases like, "it is what it is" to explain something. They use the simplest words possible to get across their ideas. And they don't bullsh*it. They say what they mean. Follow these four rules in conversation, writing and presenting and you'll become known as a dynamic communicator.

Chapter 20

Conversation Skills

Effective communication, especially in conversation, is an up-close and personal endeavor. All of the great communicators I know are also great conversationalists. As with most things, I have one great piece of common sense advice on how to become a great conversationalist: *Listen more than you speak.* When I am in a conversation, I try to spend one-third of my time speaking and two-thirds listening. I've found that this ratio works well for me.

Most people like to talk about themselves. The best way to get people to talk about themselves is to ask a lot of questions. When you meet people for the first time, ask "get to know you" questions. You know the kind of questions I'm talking about here: "What do you do?" "Where do you live?" "Are you married?" "Do you have children?"

Listen to the answers and file the information for future use. The other day, I called on an old client. Before going to see him, I thought about what I knew about him from our past conversations. Here's what I remembered. We know several people in common.

His son is a music major at Ithaca College. His company was recently acquired.

I prepared myself for our meeting by coming up with four questions: 1) How is your son doing at Ithaca? 2) Have you spoken to Jo (our mutual acquaintance) lately? 3) I saw Tom (another mutual acquaintance) the other day, have you spoken to him recently? 4) How are things going with your new company?

By asking these questions, listening and adding follow-up comments and questions, I was able to keep things moving for an hour. At the end of the hour, I was in a position to ask the two questions that were my reason for the conversation. "How are things going with your team? How can I help you?" After all, this was a sales call.

My friend Debra Fine, author of the bestseller *The Fine Art of Small Talk* calls this "going deeper." A couple of years ago, I interviewed her on my Internet talk radio show. Here is what she had to say...

"Don't be afraid to dig deeper. When you say to someone "how's work?" they're going to say 'pretty good' or 'good' or 'great' or whatever. Dig in deeper, let them know you're sincere with one more question, say something like, 'So, what's been going on with work, Bud, since the last time we talked?' Or if you say to somebody 'how were your holidays?' and they say 'great,' you can follow up by saying, 'What did you do over the holidays that you enjoyed the most?' Let them know you are sincere.

We say to our friends, 'How are you, Bud?' If you give a one-word answer like 'great,' I've got to follow up with something like, 'Bud, bring me up to date – what's been going on in your life since the last time I saw you?' Now you know that I really want to know how you are, otherwise 'how are you?' will end up meaning 'hello.' That's all it means.

By the same token, you don't want to become what I call an 'FBI agent.' That's why one follow-up question is important, but no more after that."

Debra makes some great points about the power of questions in conversation. The key here is to ask questions, listen to what people say and respond appropriately. Then file away what you've learned. I recommend writing it down so you won't forget. Review what you know about a person before visiting with him or her. This will help you prepare for the conversation by choosing the questions you want to ask.

Listening is the key to becoming a great conversationalist. Dr. Joyce Brothers makes an interesting point about listening.

"Listening, not imitation, may be the sincerest form of flattery." She's right!

When you really listen to someone, really listen, giving him or her your undivided attention, you show that you care about him or her as a human being. What could be more considerate?

The U.S. Department of Labor suggests several reasons for developing your listening skills. Developing your listening skills will help you:

- Better understand assignments and what is expected of you.
- Build rapport with co-workers, bosses and customers.
- Show support for others.
- Work better in a team-based environment.
- Resolve problems with co-workers, bosses and customers.
- Answer questions completely.
- Find the underlying meaning in what others say.

There are some generally accepted ideas about what it takes to be a good listener:

- Maintain eye contact with the person with whom you are speaking.
- Don't interrupt – except to ask a clarification question.
- Use non-verbal cues – nod your head, lean toward the other person, sit still – that indicate you are listening.
- Repeat what the other person says – to be sure you understand and to get clarification.

I have a worked out a listening-to-speaking ratio for effective conversations. Listen two-thirds of the time. Speak one-third of the time. This way, you give others more time to share their thoughts and ideas. You'll flatter them by your willingness to listen.

Listening is more than just not talking. To listen well, you need to engage mentally with the other person. You need to focus on what he or she is saying and you need to respond in a way that indicates you're paying attention.

You should listen most diligently when you find yourself disagreeing with what the other person is saying. It's easy to tune out someone with whom you disagree. When you really listen to what he or she has to say, you are not only demonstrating respect for him or her as a person, you put yourself in a position to learn something new.

Many hosts of political talk shows on television are terrible listeners. They invite people who hold opposing views to be on their show. They ask provocative questions. And then begin to argue with their guest as soon as he or she begins speaking. This may be good TV but it is a poor example of how to truly listen and engage with another person.

I read a lot. I sometimes find great information in unexpected places and that's the case when it comes to listening. Tony Hillerman and Andrew Vachss are two of my favorite novelists. To my great sorrow, Tony Hillerman has since passed away. He wrote mysteries set on the Navajo reservation in the American Southwest. Vachss writes tough-guy mysteries, most of them set in New York.

I was reading a Hillerman book called *Coyote Waits* and came across this passage:

> Jacobs was silent for a while, thinking about it, her face full of sympathy. She was a talented listener. He had noticed it before. She had all her antennae out, focused on the speaker. The world was shut out. Nothing mattered but the words she was hearing. Listening was ingrained in Navajo culture. One didn't interrupt. One waited until the speaker was finished, gave him a moment or two to consider additions, footnotes or amendments, before he responded. But even Navajos listened impatiently. Not really listening,

but framing their reply. Jean Jacobs really listened. It was flattery, and Chee knew it, but it had its effect.

I respect my books and usually don't dog-ear them to mark a page. But I dog-eared this page. I knew I would use it when I was writing about listening.

What's the message in the Hillerman passage? Listen. Don't interrupt. Let the other person finish. Don't start deciding what you're going to say until after you've listened to, and thought about, what the other person has said. Pretty good stuff to find in the middle of a mystery novel.

Andrew Vachss has another passage on good listening. Burke is one of his characters. He is a tough guy but listening is one of his strong suits...

It's not hard to get some people to talk; it's listening that takes real skill. You can't just shift to recorder mode until you confirm the channel is open and the signal is strong. Sometimes, they just need to tell you something important to them before they tell you anything important to you. It's like uncorking a bottle of wine and letting it breathe before you have a taste.

Burke's message is pretty clear, too. Focus on the other person. Let him or her take the lead. If you're patient, you'll get the information you want or need.

You might find it odd that I'm dispensing listening advice based on what I've read in mystery novels. One of Stephen Covey's *7 Habits of Highly Effective People* is, "Seek first to understand, then to be understood." Hillerman and Vachss are saying the same thing – in a more poetic style. Listen and you will better understand others. When you understand others it's a lot easier to build strong relationships with them. Listening is key to conversation and conversation is key to relationship- building. Focusing on the other person – really paying attention to what he or she is saying – is key to listening. Focus your attention on the other person, pay attention to what he or she says. Respond appropriately. Listen more than you speak. Show people that you value them and what they have to say.

Conversations happen one-to-one and in group settings. I once saw a person self-destruct in a team meeting – all because of the choice of one word. I was facilitating a meeting for a work group. Midway through the meeting, one of the participants was reporting on a project she had been working on all year.

When she showed a slide that highlighted the results that she expected this project to show, one of the other people on the team interrupted her and said, "I cannot ethically support this project."

As you can imagine, that brought the meeting to a halt. Silence reigned. It's not often that you hear someone call a colleague's ethics into question in a public forum.

Two things followed. First, the other people in the meeting began asking questions about why this person was questioning the information being presented. Most people, including the person who raised the ethics issue, had seen a preliminary version of the presentation. All the others agreed with the ideas being presented and wanted to understand the reasons behind this one person's disagreement. The individual who criticized the project spent a lot of time explaining his position and arguing his point – unsuccessfully. As best as I could tell, he was taking issue with some of the assumptions on which the study and its conclusions were based.

Second, several people called the person who leveled the criticism on his use of the word, "ethically." They felt that it was inappropriate to call a colleague's ethics into question in such a public way when he had ample opportunity to dispute the findings earlier and in private.

I intervened and did my best to provide the person who leveled the criticism the opportunity to gracefully retract his words. He stuck to his guns on the word "ethically" but could not demonstrate to anyone in the room why he felt that the conclusions being presented were unethical. After the meeting, a few people said to me, "He was accusing her of lying, of knowingly presenting false data. This wasn't the case."

The individual who leveled the ethics charge did a lot to damage himself in the eyes of his teammates. All of this could have been avoided if he had chosen his words better.

If he had said, "I don't agree with the assumptions on which you're basing your conclusions," he would have been more precise in his use of language – and he would not have hurt his reputation among team members.

I reminded the team that one of its ground rules is to keep private the conversations that occur during team meetings. I predict that this conversation – and accusation – will leak and that the person who leveled the ethics charge will suffer further damage to his reputation. All because of a poorly chosen word he refused to retract.

There are two common sense points here. First, precision in language is key to becoming an effective conversationalist. The more you find the words that exactly communicate what you want to say, the better your chances of communicating effectively. Second, avoid inflammatory words whenever possible. It is not wise to say something like, "I cannot ethically support your project," when you mean, "I disagree with the assumptions on which your conclusions are based." Be precise in your choice of words. Don't compound the use of imprecise language by using inflammatory words.

Chapter 21

Writing Skills

Good writing will set you apart and put you on the road to corporate career success. I have found that most people are poor writers. They are unclear. They ramble. Their emails, letters and reports are a series of long sentences filled with big words that don't really say anything. That's why you can catch people's attention by writing in a clear, crisp, concise manner.

I try to write like a journalist. I use short sentences with a simple subject – verb – object structure. My writing may read a little staccato-like but it communicates. People can understand my points and the reasoning behind them.

Your objective in writing at work is to communicate – not to impress others with your vocabulary. When I was speaking with my niece about my book *Straight Talk for Success* at her graduation party, I said that I tried for an "avuncular hip" writing style. She said, "What does that mean?" I replied, "Avuncular means uncle-like. I wanted to sound like a hip uncle to people reading the book." She came back with an excellent question, "Why didn't you just say so?"

She was right. Everybody knows what "uncle-like" means. A lot of people, including *cum laude* graduates, don't know what "avuncular" means. I was just showing off my vocabulary. As a result, I didn't communicate effectively. This was an example from oral communication but the same thinking applies to writing.

Write in short, simple sentences. Use the simplest words you can to get across your point, while still being accurate. Write fast. Get your thoughts on paper or the computer screen as quickly as you can. Then edit and rewrite until you've said exactly what you want to say. One of my first bosses always told me that rewriting is the secret to good writing.

Write with the reader in mind. I like a conversational style. It communicates better and engages the reader. Stilted, over-formal writing doesn't communicate. In fact, it tends to put off the reader. Read aloud what you've written to get a feel for how it will sound in your reader's mind. If it sounds clear and inviting, you've done a good job.

Spelling counts. Correct spelling does two things for you. First, it shows that you have a good command of the language. Second and more important, correct spelling shows that you respect both yourself and the reader. Misspelled words stick out like sore thumbs.

Don't just spell-check your documents. Proof them. Spell-check often won't pick up improper usage in words like "your" and "you're," "hear" and "here," and "their" and "there."

The same holds true for punctuation. Make sure that you know how to properly use periods, question marks, commas, colons, semicolons, exclamation marks, quotation marks and apostrophes. If you're not sure about punctuation rules, spend some time on the Internet learning proper usage.

I like the Poynter Institute for good information about writing. While the information on their site www.poynter.org is aimed at journalists, there is a lot of helpful information about writing and editing there – especially in the article in "Tip Sheets," which can be found by clicking on the "Reporting, Writing and Editing" button.

Choose words carefully. I remember reading a column in an airline in-flight magazine on jargon. Even though it's been several years, I still remember it. The author began by saying that he has a folder of memos with obtuse language that he has collected over the years. He shared one memo that a friend sent to him. I was so struck by the language that I saved it on my hard drive. The guy who wrote the memo said he was going to "map the handoffs and all processes in a combined swim lanes uber-process." I'm pretty hip to a lot of business jargon, since I see it every day. I must admit, however, that "swim lanes uber-process" was a new one.

As I'm writing this, I'm reminded of an IBM commercial I saw recently. A guy walks into a large, dimly lit conference room where he sees no tables and chairs and about twenty people lying on the floor. He says, "What are you guys doing?" Someone answers, "We're ideating." He says, "What's that?" Someone responds, "Coming up with new ways of doing things." He says, "Why don't you just call it that?"

Interestingly enough, the word ideating sounds a lot like a made-up word to me. I expected spell-check to flag it. It didn't. So I guess I'm behind the times on some of my business jargon. Even so, I think saying that you're "coming up with new ways of doing things," is much more clear than saying that you're "ideating." But what do I know?

This brings me to the "Bafflegab Thesaurus." I first saw the "Bafflegab Thesaurus" back in the 1970s. It's made a comeback lately, only this time it's called "Buzzwords for Business Writing." Whatever you choose to call it, it's very clever. It points out just how much jargon has taken over business communication.

Here's how it works. When you're stuck in your writing, this quick guide helps you create phrases that will make you sound as if you know what you're talking about. It's simple. Think of any three-digit number and then select the corresponding buzzword from each column. Voila! You're done.

Here's an example. The three-digit number 257 produces "systematized logistical projection." You can drop this phrase into

COLUMN I	COLUMN II	COLUMN III
0. Integrated	0. Management	0. Options
1. Heuristic	1. Organizational	1. Flexibility
2. Systematized	2. Monitored	2. Capability
3. Parallel	3. Reciprocal	3. Mobility
4. Functional	4. Digital	4. Programming
5. Responsive	5. Logistical	5. Scenarios
6. Optional	6. Transitional	6. Time-phase
7. Synchronized	7. Incremental	7. Projection
8. Compatible	8. Third-generation	8. Hardware
9. Futuristic	9. Policy	9. Contingency

almost any report. It has a ring of decisive, knowledgeable authority. Of course, no one will have the remotest idea of what you're talking about. But that's OK. The important thing is that *they aren't about to admit it.*

You realize, of course, that I'm joking here. While "systematized logistical projection" may sound good, it really means nothing. The best writers use small words, simple sentences and the active voice of verbs. Never use this buzzword generator in your business communication.

There is a common sense point here. In conversation, writing and presenting, use simple, straight-forward language that is likely to be understood by the person or people with whom you are communicating. Put yourself in the place of others. Use words and language that they are likely to understand.

Your writing can make you appear more intelligent or less intelligent than you really are. I think appearing more intelligent is better. Take modifiers for example. How you use modifiers can have a big impact on the impression you make with your writing.

When you use modifiers incorrectly, they actually muddy your message and suggest carelessness on your part. Here are two of the most common errors in using modifiers, along with ways to avoid them.

A **misplaced modifier** that modifies the wrong word can cause confusion for your reader. Here's an example: *Sheila almost worked until midnight.*

To say that "Sheila *almost* worked" makes her look like a slacker. The writer probably wanted to say that Sheila worked late—until *almost* midnight. The placement of the modifier "almost" makes a big difference in the meaning of the sentence. To avoid such misunderstandings, be sure your modifiers are close to the words they describe.

The **dangling modifier** is a common error in which the modified word is either far from the modifier or missing completely, making the sentence unclear or even preposterous. Here is an example: *Racing recklessly down the street, the houses became a blur.*

In this instance, it appears that the houses were "racing down the street" – an unlikely event. To repair such an error, the writer must clearly indicate who or what was racing: *Racing recklessly down the street, I saw only a blur of houses.*

Another repair turns the modifying phrase into a clause by adding a subject: *As I raced recklessly down the street, the houses became a blur.*

Always check your modifiers to make sure they are modifying the right words. The result will be clearer communication. Many people often misplace modifiers causing their written communication to suffer, making them appear as if they don't understand the basic rules of grammar – and making them seem less intelligent than they are.

I find that the word "only" is often used incorrectly as a modifier. Take a look at these two sentences. Sentence 1: You can only eat after you have washed your hands. Sentence 2: You can eat only after you have washed your hands.

Sentence 1 means that eating is the only thing that you can do after you've washed your hands. Sentence 2 means that you cannot eat until you have washed your hands. In my experience, many people will use sentence 1 when they mean to convey the message of sentence 2. Mistakes like this can cast a negative light on your written communication skills.

Take the time to read what you write with a critical eye. Make sure that the words you use as modifiers enhance, not detract from, your communication. Be especially careful with the word "only." It is the modifier most often used incorrectly.

Chapter 22

Presentation Skills

Many a career has been built on one good presentation. Presentations are your chance to shine. Unfortunately, many people fear presenting in front of an audience. Their fear robs them of the advantages and opportunities presentations afford.

Don't let this happen to you. Presenting is like any other process. It can be broken down into a series of manageable steps. Master the following steps and you'll become a great presenter…

1. Determine your message.

Begin by determining what you have to say. Get crystal clear on the message you have for the audience.

2. Analyze your audience.

Why are they there? How much do they know about your topic? Are they familiar with any jargon you might use? What is their general attitude towards you and the information you will be communicating?

3. Organize your information for impact.

I always start at the end. I write my closing first. I use this closing to help me choose the information I am going to include in my talk. I ask myself, "Does this information add to my main point?" If the answer is yes, I leave it in. If the answer is no, I take it out. Then I write my opening. I design my opening statements to do two things – get the attention of others, and then tell them what I will be telling them in my talk. Once the closing and opening are written, I simply fill in the content.

4. Create supporting visuals.

Once I've decided what I want to say and how I want to say it, I develop my visuals. Your visuals should support your presentation – not drive it. There is nothing more boring than watching and listening to someone reading slides.

5. Practice out loud.

This is the most important point of all. As an early mentor told me, "Bud, preparation makes up for a lack of talent." It also enhances your natural talent. Never skip this step. If you do, you will likely do a poor talk. And while a poor presentation generally is not a career killer, it is a missed opportunity.

Stories are a powerful way to communicate in presentations. We all learn through stories. I've come up with a simple three-step formula to create powerful stories that will help you make your point.

First, identify your truth – something that in your heart of hearts you know to be "true." Second, think of the critical experiences you've had that have led you to this "truth." Third, shape those experiences into a story that you can tell at the drop of a hat.

Here's an example of how I have used this formula. It's a real story that I often tell in my talks.

"One of the things that I know to be true is that if I am going to be a good communicator, I must meet other people where they are, not where I would like them to be. Let me tell you how I know this.

Several years ago, I had an assignment to conduct a team-building session for a manufacturing plant manager and his staff. The client was a friend of mine. I knew him well.

I arrived at his office about 5:00 the afternoon of the day before our session. He said, 'Do you have an agenda for tomorrow's meeting?'

I said, 'Well, first we'll do A, then B, followed by C. We'll finish up with D.'

He said, 'Do you have an agenda?'

At first, I thought he hadn't been listening to what I just said, so I repeated myself: 'First, we'll do A, then B, followed by C. We'll finish up with D.'

He said, 'Yes, I know. That's what you just said. Do you have an agenda?'

At that point, it dawned on me that he was looking for a

printed agenda. I said 'No, but we really don't need one. I've done a lot of meetings like this. It will go fine.'

He said, 'I'm not comfortable winging it.' So we created an agenda using PowerPoint.

The next day, the meeting went off without a hitch. We followed the agenda that I had in my head and he had on the PowerPoint slide. Everyone agreed that it was one of the best meetings of this type that they had ever attended.

My client said, 'It was a great meeting but I still think we were lucky because we were winging it.'

On the flight home, I thought about what had happened. He thought we were winging it. I thought we were following a well-thought-out plan. The difference was that he needed more structure than I do. The piece of paper with the agenda was very important to him and his sense of order. To me, the paper wasn't necessary because I knew in my head what to do and how to do it.

It became clear that if I want to influence not just this client, but other clients as well, I have to adapt my communication style to theirs. From that day on, I modify my communication style to meet the needs of the other person."

As you read the story, you can see how I used my 1 - 2 - 3 formula to construct a story that I can use any time I want to help people see and learn the importance of using stories to make a key point.

Presentation anxiety – stage fright – can be the death knell for an otherwise great talk. We all get nervous before a talk. Being nervous, however, doesn't have to mean you'll do a bad talk. You can make your nerves work for you.

Presentation anxiety is a response to fear of doing a poor talk. It shows up in a number of ways: blushing, shaking, stuttering, sweating. It will lead you to feel as if you're not making sense, or worse, to lose the thread of your talk.

I'm sure you know the story about the survey that asked people to name their greatest fear. Public speaking came in first, by a large margin. Death was fourth. So, if we are to believe the results of this survey, most people would rather die than stand up and give a talk.

I make speeches for a living and I still get nervous. In fact, if I'm not a little nervous, I start to worry that I'll be flat and deliver an unenthusiastic talk. Over the years, I've developed a few tricks that I use to calm my nerves before a big presentation:

Practice your talk out loud. This will help you get comfortable with your material and your delivery.

Think good thoughts. Imagine yourself succeeding beyond your wildest dreams. Imagine that you will get a standing ovation for your talk.

Get there early. This way, you'll be able to set up your computer and run through your slides one last time.

Greet people as they arrive. Exchange a few words with them. This will help you make a good first impression with members of the audience. It will also help you get control of your nerves because you'll feel more comfortable speaking to a group of people you know rather than a group of strangers.

Take a deep breath before you begin. This will calm you, help center you and give you enough air to get through your opening.

Move. When you begin your presentation, move around. Use body movement to release some of your nervous energy.

Just chat. Think of your presentation as a conversation. There might be 10, 25 or 100 people in the audience. But in terms of real communication, there are only two people in the room: you and a single listener.

Ask questions during your talk. This will help you build a dialogue and a participatory feeling. I try to make at least one-quarter or as much as one-half of my talk a discussion with the audience. In this way, it's less of a speech and more of an expanded conversation with every person in the room.

Don't worry if you make a mistake. To begin with, most people won't realize that you made the mistake. Second, realize the audience is with you. They've all been there and know that presenting can be nerve-wracking. Most people in the audience will be pulling for you to do a good job.

Presentations are an opportunity to shine. Don't let stage fright rob you of this opportunity. The tips above should help you deal with presentation anxiety. One piece of advice, however, is paramount here: practice, practice, practice!

Section 7

Relationship
Building

R elationship building is the fourth competency you have to master to become a career success. No matter how self-confident you are, how good you are at creating positive personal impact, how great a performer or dynamic a communicator you are, you won't succeed if you can't build strong, lasting and mutually beneficial relationships.

Pat Wiesner was the publisher of *Colorado Business* Magazine and wrote the "On Management" column. A couple of years ago, he wrote a great column entitled, "The Biggest Management Sin of All: How to Lose Your Job or at Least Deserve to Lose It."

The biggest sin? Demeaning people. Pat says, "My belief is that if we get caught shouting at people, demeaning them in any way, we should be fired. On the spot."

I agree. And this holds for everyone – not just people in leadership and management positions. Raising your voice and demeaning people is not only poor leadership, it's one of the hallmarks of interpersonally incompetent people.

Belittling and intimidating, or otherwise demeaning, people isn't just nasty. It destroys their self-esteem and self-confidence. Pat says, "Once you have made someone feel really negative about himself, how long would it take to reverse that feeling? Pretty tough to do." I believe that interpersonally competent people help others build – not destroy – their self-confidence.

The interpersonally incompetent seem to believe that the way to feel good about themselves is to make others feel bad about themselves. That's why they engage in demeaning and bullying behavior.

This is simply not true. The title of one of the first self-help books I read – published by Thomas Harris in 1969, *I'm OK, You're OK* – says it best. Interpersonally competent people come from an "I'm OK, You're OK" place. Bullies and demeaning people come from an "I'm OK, You're Not OK" place.

Interpersonally competent people realize that we're all OK. They work hard to meet people where they are and to build strong relationships with all the people in their lives.

Treat people with kindness and respect. Help them enhance their feelings of self-esteem. Do what you can to build their self-confidence. If you do, you'll be known as an interpersonally competent person – and interpersonally competent people are welcome wherever they go.

Interpersonal competence will help you create rich relationships that last a lifetime. In *The Little Black Book of Connections*, Jeffrey Gitomer offers the best piece of common sense advice I've ever seen on relationships:

> "Everyone wants to be rich. Although most people think being rich is about having money, rich is a description for everything but money. Rich relationships lead to much more than money. They lead to success, fulfillment and wealth."

As you probably expect, there are a few common sense points associated with interpersonal competence. Understand yourself. Think about what makes you tick. When you're working with others, think about what makes them tick. If they're different from you, decide what you need to do to be better able to communicate with them. Second, do things for others– and don't keep score. Good things will come your way, often from unexpected sources. Build relationships by being willing to do for others whether or not they are willing to do for you. Finally, when you are in conflict, look for where you agree with the other person. Use these small places of agreements to build a mutually acceptable resolution to your conflict.

Interpersonally competent people are good at building strong, lasting relationships. My best advice for relationship building is to "give with no expectation of anything in return."

I know that it seems that the world works on *quid pro quo*. People expect it. That's why when you do something nice and unexpected for others and expect nothing in return, you'll be on your way to building strong relationships with them.

Chapter 23

Get to Know Yourself

Interpersonally competent people understand themselves. They use this self-understanding to better understand others and build and maintain long-term, mutually beneficial relationships with the important people in their lives. If you want to understand others and build strong relationships, you have to understand yourself. Take a few minutes and answer these questions...

When I need to recharge my batteries, do I prefer to be around other people, or do I prefer to be by myself?

Do I like to take in information in a structured step-by-step manner or do I prefer getting a lot of information all at once and figuring out the connections for myself?

Do I make decisions with my heart or with my head?

Do I like to resolve things quickly or do I like to wait to the last minute to commit to a course of action?

You probably lean to one or the other of the choices in the four questions above. Once you know your answers to these questions, think about the people around you. How are they similar to you? How are they different?

Let's take a Friday night, for example. You and your partner or spouse are invited to a party. You've both had a long week and you're tired. If you are the type of person who recharges your batteries by engaging in solitary activities, make sure you find time for yourself. If your spouse or partner is the opposite, let him or her go to the party on his or her own. He or she won't even miss you – there will be enough people at the party to recharge his or her batteries, and you'll get the precious alone time that you need.

If you take in information in a highly structured step-by-step manner, you'll have a difficult time dealing with people who are big-picture thinkers and who make intuitive leaps. You like to have information presented in a 1, 2, 2a, 2b, 3, 3a, 3b, 3c manner. Big-picture people, those who make intuitive leaps, will be all over the place – 1, 4a, 3b, 2, 2d. You'll be frustrated because of what you perceive as their lack of structure and discipline. They are likely to be frustrated with you because of what they perceive as your lack of imagination. Both of you need to adapt your communication style to be able to communicate with each other.

If you make decisions with your heart, you'll have a tough time convincing someone who makes decisions with his or her head to do something because "it is the right thing to do." Instead, you'll need to figure out the rational, logical reasons for what you want to do if you are going to convince a "head" person to go along with your ideas.

If you like to resolve things quickly, you'll be frustrated by others who wait till the last minute to commit. If you want to build a strong relationship with these people, you need to help them understand the urgency in committing to a course of action. On the other hand, you might find it beneficial to take a step back and see if you're creating artificial deadlines just to satisfy your needs.

It's important to know yourself. It's more important to know how you are similar and different from others so that you can use this knowledge to become more influential with them. The more you can understand your style and needs, the better you'll understand others' style and needs. The more you can adapt your preferred style to another person, the better able you will be to build relationships and resolve conflict.

Chapter 24

Pay It Forward

C arolyn Hawver is a friend and client. A while back, we had a meeting scheduled for 10:00 on a Thursday. At 7:00 that morning, I received an email from her that said:

> Bud:
> I know we have a meeting scheduled for 10:00, but I am having computer problems and the IT guy can see me at 10:00 only. It should take only about 15 minutes. Can we move our meeting to 10:15? I don't want you to have to waste your time while the IT guy looks at my computer.
> I'm sorry to do this, but I hope you understand.
> Carolyn

Sure, I understood. Emergencies, especially IT emergencies, happen all the time. And IT emergencies usually need to get fixed as soon as possible – they're important and urgent.

I understood and I really appreciated Carolyn's email. In the scheme of things, 15 minutes is no big deal. I know people whose offices are near hers. I could have visited with them and not wasted my time.

But Carolyn took the time to tell me that she would be running late. By her email, she paid it forward. She showed that she was aware of, and cared about, my time. That's one reason she is an interpersonally competent person and good at building relationships. She is aware of how her actions affect other people. She does what she can to avoid inconveniencing others.

If you want to build strong, collaborative relationships with the people in your life, follow Carolyn's example. Pay it forward. Be aware of how your actions affect others. Do everything you can to not inconvenience them. When you do inconvenience another person, apologize and promise to try to avoid doing it in the future.

Here's another example. In a recent blog post, I featured an article in *Self Improvement Magazine* by Tricia Molloy called "CRAVE Your Goals!" I featured it because I thought Tricia presented an interesting and unique way of looking at goals that would benefit my readers. I also hoped that I could give Tricia some exposure to an audience she might not normally reach. I didn't know Tricia at the time.

The day after the post went up I got this comment from her...

"Hi, Bud:

Thanks for sharing my 'CRAVE Your Goals!' system with your readers. I enjoyed reading your comments about each step.

Tristan's comment about common sense not equaling common practice is so true. People often think these practices are too easy to work. They assume achieving goals always takes hard work and a bit of suffering. What I suggest is to start with the one CRAVE step that resonates the most – like cleaning out some clutter or using an affirmation – and that will give you the energy and clarity to try another step until all five steps become a habit.

To more common sense!

Namaste, Tricia."

Tricia and I are friends now – all because I took a little of my time to feature her article on my blog. This was a win/win/win/win. My readers benefited, Tricia benefited, Tristan, the publisher of *Self Improvement Magazine* benefited, and I benefited – all because I did something with no expectation of anything in return. It's karmic, really. It seems that very often you get things back when you least expect to.

Strong relationships have no *quid pro quo*. In a strong relationship, all parties do things willingly for one another, for the benefit of the individuals involved and for the benefit of the relationship. It's similar to the idea behind the hit movie *Pay it Forward*.

When you pay it forward in a relationship, you demonstrate that the relationship and the other person or persons is important to you. You build goodwill by being the one who is willing to go first. In my coaching, speaking and consulting business, I've found that paying it forward has helped me build solid, long-term relationships with clients. Try it. It will work for you, too.

Interpersonally competent people build relationships by doing for others. They don't keep score. They know that in the long run, good things will come to them if they do good things for others.

I am a member of the Creating WE Institute, a group of people with multi-disciplinary expertise working to create new forms of engagement and innovation in the workplace. We have published a book *42 Rules for Creating WE*. I contributed three rules. One is called "There is No Quid Pro Quo in WE." I believe this. Giving with no expectation of return is the best way to build strong, lasting, mutually beneficial relationships.

Paying it forward is one way to make regular deposits in your emotional bank accounts. I first became aware of the concept of an emotional bank account about 20 years ago when I read Stephen Covey's *The 7 Habits of Highly Effective People.*

Interpersonally competent people make regular deposits in the emotional bank accounts they have with all the people in their lives.

In the spring of 2008, a major league baseball team made a huge deposit into the emotional bank account it has with several different groups of people.

The New York Yankees traveled from Florida to Virginia to play an exhibition game against the Virginia Tech baseball team. They did this to support the Hokie Spirit Memorial Fund that was created to cover grief counseling, memorials and other costs for the victims of the Virginia Tech shootings and their families. In 2007, a Virginia Tech student Seung-Hui Cho killed 32 people in two campus buildings before committing suicide.

I'm not a Yankee fan but I remembered this game whenever George Steinbrenner, the Yankees' late owner, did something outlandish that ended up in the news. The emotional bank account I have with the Yankees received a major deposit that day.

The emotional bank account that the Yankees have with the Virginia Tech community got an even bigger deposit that day. The Yankees helped raise a lot of money for a very sad and deserving cause. They brought some happiness and light to a campus struggling with the memory of the shootings.

Finally, the Yankees made a big deposit in the emotional bank account of anyone who is a baseball fan. Compassion and a willingness to pitch in and help go a long way in filling emotional bank accounts.

Most of us don't get to make such grand gestures. We can choose to make regular deposits into the emotional bank accounts we have with the people in our lives. There are six ways you can do this for people important to you.

1. **Make a sincere effort to understand others.** Figure out what's important to all of the key people in your life. Make what's important to them important to you.

2. **Pay attention to the little things.** Little things are big things in relationships.

3. **Keep your commitments.** Every time you do what you say

you'll do, you make an emotional bank account deposit. Fail to keep your word and you'll be making a withdrawal.

4. **Be clear on what you want and expect from another person.** This makes it easier for the other person to give it to you. When you take the time to gain clarity on what others want, it's easier to keep your commitments.

5. **Be honest.** Make sure your words and actions are in sync. Remember what Mark Twain said: "Always tell the truth. That way, you don't have to remember anything."

6. **Apologize when you make a withdrawal.** Often, a sincere apology will be enough of an emotional bank account deposit to offset your withdrawal. This works only for the occasional withdrawal. You can't continue to break your word or miss your commitments and think that an apology will keep your emotional bank account full.

The common sense point here is simple. Make regular deposits to the emotional bank accounts you have with all the important people in your life. Keep your balances high. This way, you won't be overdrawn when you have to make the occasional withdrawal.

Here's another story to illustrate my point. I'm a Pittsburgh guy. I grew up in Ambridge, just 15 miles from where the confluence of the Monongahela and Allegheny rivers forms the Ohio River. I am a lifelong Pittsburgh Steeler fan.

Displaced Pittsburgh guys like me have a love affair with their hometown and its football team. A while back, a friend of mine sent me an article about Art Rooney, the founder of the Pittsburgh Steelers. He's gone now but the people in Pittsburgh remember him fondly.

The story takes place in a funeral home. Kathleen Rooney, Art's wife of more than 50 years, had just passed away. A guy by the name of Dan Lackner, who worked in the Steelers' office when he was in high school, went to pay his respects.

While he was there, he ran into friend whose father, a retired Pittsburgh fireman, had just passed away. He paid his respects to his friend's father. There were no people or flowers in the old fireman's visitation room. The son said that his dad had outlived all his friends. He wasn't surprised that very few people had come to pay their respects. In fact, he wasn't even sure if it made any sense to have a viewing.

You have to understand that, in Pittsburgh, everybody goes to viewings at funeral homes. When my grandmother passed away, I saw people I hadn't seen since I graduated from high school 40 years earlier. They read the obituaries and showed up. She spent the last 15 years of her life in Florida. Nevertheless, members of her church in Pittsburgh came to pray for her the night before her burial. So, in Pittsburgh, an empty visitation room with a casket and no mourners is a sad thing.

As the story goes, Art Rooney, mourning his wife, noticed Dan Lackner coming out of the other room. He asked who was there. Lackner told him the story. Mr. Rooney was a generous man. He immediately went to the room to pay his respects to a man he had never met.

As you might imagine, there was no shortage of flowers for Mrs. Rooney. Mr. Rooney began telling the delivery men to take them to the Lackner family's room. They ended up with quite a collection of bouquets.

When famous Steelers Joe Greene, Terry Bradshaw and Mel Blount came to pay their respects to Mrs. Rooney, Art sent them to the other room to pay their respects to the fireman. He told them to be sure to sign the guest book. Art sent Pete Rozelle, the NFL Commissioner, back to pay his respects, along with Al Davis, owner of the Oakland Raiders, and Pete Flaherty, the mayor of Pittsburgh.

The article ended with these words: "Everybody who was anybody in the National Football League had signed the fireman's guest book. That's just the way Art Rooney was. That visitor's book might be worth something one of these days."

That was the way Art Rooney was. He was a man who did things for others, even if they could do nothing for him. Interpersonally competent people do this. They are kind and generous. They know that generosity is the secret to relationship building.

As Ralph Waldo Emerson said, "You cannot do a kindness too soon, for you never know how soon it will be too late."

Chapter 25

Use Conflict Constructively

Interpersonally competent people resolve conflict in a positive manner. No matter how interpersonally competent you are, or how easygoing, you will inevitably find yourself in conflict. People won't always agree with you and you won't always agree with others.

I know a little bit about conflict resolution. It was the topic of my dissertation at Harvard. Way back in the 1970s, Ken Thomas and Ralph Kilmann developed an instrument to measure a person's tendencies when in a conflict situation.

They came up with five predominant conflict styles: Competing, Collaborating, Compromising, Accommodating and Avoiding. Their research suggests that all five are appropriate depending on the situation.

In my experience, however, I have found that the Collaborating style is the best default mode. When you collaborate with others to resolve conflict, you focus on meeting both your needs and needs of the other person. I like this style because it helps bring together a variety of viewpoints to get the best solution.

When you collaborate, neither person is likely to feel as if he or she won or lost. Also, collaborating with the person or persons with whom you are in conflict creates the opportunity for you to work together to build a solution that best addresses everyone's concerns.

I find that when I work collaboratively with someone, I focus on our similarities, rather than on our differences. This creates a bond that not only helps us get through our conflict but helps us strengthen our relationship.

Interpersonally competent people are adept at resolving conflict in a positive manner. Collaboration is the best choice of the five most common handling styles. When you collaborate with others – especially those you are in conflict with – you not only are likely to resolve your conflict in a positive manner, you strengthen your relationship with the other person. It's a win-win.

As I mentioned, my favorite method for dealing with conflict is counter-intuitive. By definition, conflict is a state of disagreement. When I'm in conflict with someone, however, instead of focusing on where we disagree, I focus on where we agree.

This is a great way to resolve conflict positively and strengthen relationships. As we all know, conflict often leads to a deterioration of relationships. That's a no-brainer. First, you get to resolve conflict positively. Second, you strengthen your relationships.

I look for any small point of agreement and then try to build on it. I find that it is easier to reach a larger agreement when I build from a point of small agreement, rather than attempting to tear down the other person's points I don't agree with.

Most people don't do this. They get caught up in trying to prove their point. They hold on to it more strongly when someone else attacks it. If you turn around the discussion and say, "Let's focus where we agree and see if we can build something from there," you make the situation less personal. Now, you're both working to figure out a mutually agreeable solution to a disagreement. You're not tearing down one another's arguments just to get your way. Try it. It works.

President Obama demonstrated this in his first speech to a joint session of Congress. As he was winding up his talk, he said…

"I know that we haven't agreed on every issue thus far, and there are surely times in the future when we will part ways. But I also know that every American who is sitting here tonight loves this country and wants it to succeed. That must be the starting point for every debate we have in the coming months, and where we return after those debates are done. That is the foundation on which the American people expect us to build common ground.

And if we do – if we come together and lift this nation from the depths of this crisis, if we put our people back to work and restart the engine of our prosperity, if we confront without fear the challenges of our time and summon that enduring spirit of an America that does not quit, then someday years from now our children can tell their children that this was the time when we performed, in the words that are carved into this very chamber, 'something worthy to be remembered.' Thank you, God bless you, and may God bless the United States of America."

Regardless of your political views, the President was right on with this one. When you come together with the people you are in conflict with by identifying some point you agree on, you put yourself in the position to begin building a resolution to the conflict – one that is likely to be better than either side's opening position. And by working together, you'll be strengthening your relationship. This will facilitate even more effective conflict resolution down the road. Look for common ground. When you find it, build on it. It's a great way to resolve conflict that enhances, rather than destroys, relationships.

Be assertive, not aggressive. You build stronger relationships that way. Here's a true story. Frontier Flight 862, Denver to Phoenix. I get on late because I'm on standby for an earlier flight. I have a middle seat, 14B. When I arrive at row 14, there are women sitting in seats A and C. I say hello, stow my bags and get into my seat.

The woman in 14A smiles at me and looks at the book I have in my hand and says, "That looks like an interesting book." I'm reading Laura Lowell's *42 Rules of Marketing*. We chat a minute about the book and then lapse into some general conversation.

Her name is Cheryl Munsey. As it turns out, Cheryl and I know a few people in common. And she's very personable. We chat the whole time the plane is taxiing and through take-off.

As soon as the plane is in the air, the woman in 14C rings the flight attendant call button. The flight attendant comes on the loud speaker and says, "We are still in our ascent. Will the person who rang his or her call button turn it off until we reach our cruising altitude? Leave it on only if it's a real emergency."

14C leaves the light on. I'm worried that she might be ill. The flight attendant struggles down the aisle. When she arrives at our row, 14C says, "I need a pair of headphones. These people are talking too much and driving me crazy." As she is saying this, she is removing ear plugs.

I feel bad. I tend to speak softly in enclosed places like airplanes and was surprised that our conversation was annoying her – especially when she was wearing ear plugs. I say to 14C, "I apologize if we were annoying you. I didn't realize we were speaking so loudly." She says, "I was trying to sleep," and puts on the headphones that she got from the flight attendant.

Not a minute later, she rings the call button again. When the flight attendant comes back, she says, "I need another pair. These earphones aren't drowning out these people." I thought this was kind of peculiar, as Cheryl and I were stunned by what had happened and really hadn't said anything since her original complaint that we were speaking too loudly.

All of this should just go into one of those irritating, bizarre moments in life files and be forgotten. It makes a point, however, about personal responsibility and interpersonal competence.

The woman in 14C never told Cheryl and me that we were

disturbing her sleep. Instead, she chose to complain to the flight attendant about our conversation. It came across to both Cheryl and me as a hostile gesture. We both wondered why she just didn't ask us to speak more softly. That's what an interpersonally competent person would have done. That's what someone who was taking responsibility for herself and her needs would have done.

It's called being assertive. Assertive people stand up for their rights but do it in such a way as not to offend other people. Passive people let others trample on them and don't stand up for their rights. Aggressive people get what they want but at the expense of others. In this case, 14C was being aggressive.

Two common sense points here: One, take responsibility for yourself. Tell people how you feel. Don't let others do things that make your life unpleasant. Two, stand up for yourself in an assertive, non-aggressive way.

Chapter 26

Be a Team Player

You can build strong relationships by becoming a team player. Focus on the success of your colleagues, your immediate work team and your company. When they win, you win. That's why it's important to become a team player.

Here are the characteristics of team players…

Technical Competence. You can't be a fully contributing member of a team if you are not technically competent. You need to be able to do your job and do it well. This means keeping up on developments in your area of expertise. I always suggest to my coaching clients that they become their company's go-to person in their specialized area. When you're a true expert, you can help others with their questions, problems and concerns. When you consistently help colleagues, you become known as a team player – someone everyone wants to work with and have on their team.

Sharing Orientation. Good team players are willing to share their time and expertise. We all need a little help every once in a while. When you demonstrate you're willing to help others, they'll help you when the time comes. And believe me, there will be times in your corporate climb when you'll need help.

Good Interpersonal Skills. Good team players understand themselves. They use their self-awareness to better understand others. When you take the time to understand others, you're more aware of how to help them – and your team. Good team players listen more than they speak. They focus on turning tense situations into opportunities for collaboration and problem solving.

Self Reliant. Good team players take responsibility for themselves and their work. They focus on doing their job to the best of their ability and trust that their colleagues will do the same. Successful teams know that they can count on every member to carry his or her weight and that the collective effort will yield great results.

Focus on Stakeholders. No team exists in a vacuum. Most teams have several constituencies who are affected by their work. Good team members keep a constant focus on the needs of their stakeholders. They encourage teammates to do the same. Satisfied stakeholders help you create a reputation as a high-performing team.

Welcomes and Uses Feedback. Good team players know that they can always get better. They seek feedback from other team members. They listen carefully to the feedback they receive and they incorporate suggestions into their behavior. When you solicit feedback and use it, the people on your team will see you as someone who is interested in becoming a high performer and contributing to your team's reputation as a high performing team.

Meet Commitments. Good team players do what they say they'll do. People know that they can count on them. If they find that circumstances are preventing them from meeting a commitment, they notify the people who will be affected right away.

Honest. Good team players tell the truth. They are candid and courageous. Their team members know that they can count on them to be truthful. On the other hand, they never use honesty as an excuse for being hurtful. Good team members don't say malicious things in the guise of honesty. They use the truth to help move the team forward.

Initiative. Good team players look for things that need to be done – and then they do them. They don't wait to be told what to do. They volunteer for the tough jobs and do them well. They are one step ahead, anticipating needs and addressing them.

Trusting. Good team members trust their colleagues. They expect them to do what they say they will do. This trust is generally rewarded. When others feel trusted, they do their best to live up to their commitments.

Trustworthy. Good team members act in a way that lets colleagues know that they can be trusted. Besides meeting commitments, they keep confidences. They don't gossip. They may argue about team decisions in the privacy of the team but they publicly support all team decisions.

Consensus Builder. Good team members look for ways to resolve differences. They focus on points of agreement and use them to build solutions to problems. They solicit input to ensure that all sides of an issue are aired. Then they look for solutions acceptable to the entire team.

Empathy. Good team players work hard to understand the views of others, especially those people they disagree with. They focus on understanding the situations that give rise to others' points of view. They put themselves in the place of others so that they can better understand them.

Respect. Good team members never dismiss anyone out-of-hand. They believe that every human being has value and is entitled to their respect, regardless of where they stand in the hierarchy.

Commitment to the Team's Success. Good team members put "we" before "me." They commit to their team's success. They make personal sacrifices to ensure that the team meets its objectives and commitments.

Focus on Task and Process. Good team members focus not only on what the team needs to accomplish, but on how the team accomplishes what it sets out to do. They pay attention to how the team works together and offer suggestions for better working relationships within the team.

Humility. Good team members realize that they are part of something greater than themselves. The realization keeps them humble. They keep a level head even when they are singled out for their contributions. They know that the entire team is responsible for their team's success.

Supportive. Good team members are always willing to help and support colleagues. They offer their support in getting the work done as well as their moral supports. Their team members see them as someone to whom they can turn when things get tough.

Active Listening. Good team members listen. They pay attention to what is being said and the emotions behind the words. They ask questions to make sure they understand. They realize that human communication is an imperfect process and work extra hard to make sure that they are receiving the same message that is being sent.

Flexibility. Good team members realize that stuff happens and when it does, the best plans might need to be changed. They are willing to go with the flow and pick up the slack. They are not rigid and react to sudden changes in a cool and calm way.

Example. Good team members set a positive example for their teammates. They conduct themselves with integrity. They respect colleagues. They always do their best. They help teammates and the team be better than they think they can be.

These are my thoughts on what it takes to be a great team player. If you are a great team player, you will build the strong, lasting, mutually beneficial relationships that help you in your corporate climb.

Section 8

In Conclusion –
Knowing Is Not
Enough

E arly in this book, I discussed personal responsibility. I want to revisit that idea. Personal responsibility means using this material once you learn it. I wrote this book to provide you with useful information and knowledge on becoming a success in your career and life. But as the U.S. Steel pencils my father used to bring home from work said, "Knowing is not enough."

I've tried to present this material in a way that provides you with some ideas of what to do to become a success in your life and career. It's up to you to think about what's here and decide if and how you are going to use it. That's what personal responsibility is all about.

A Message to Garcia is one of the best works on personal responsibility. It is an inspirational essay written in 1899 by Elbert Hubbard. It has been made into two movies, reprinted as a pamphlet and book, translated into 37 languages and was well-known in American popular and business culture until the middle of the twentieth century. It was originally published as a filler without a title in the March 1899 issue of *Philistine* magazine.

A Message to Garcia celebrates the initiative of a soldier who accomplished a difficult mission. "He asked no questions, made no objections, requested no help, and accomplished the mission." The soldier was Andrew Summers Rowan, West Point class of 1881.

The essay suggests that readers should apply this attitude to their lives as an avenue to success. Its wide popularity at the time reflected the appeal of self-reliance and energetic problem-solving in American culture. Its "don't ask questions, get the job done" message was often used by business leaders as a motivational message to their employees. It was given to every sailor and Marine in both WWI and WWII and was often memorized by schoolchildren.

The essay is about an event in the Spanish-American War in 1898. As the American army prepared to invade the Spanish colony of Cuba, it needed to contact the leader of the Cuban insurgents Calixto Iniguez Garcia. Garcia had been fighting the Spanish for Cuban independence since 1868 and sought the help of the United States.

Here are some selected excerpts from *A Message to Garcia*:

"In all this Cuban business there is one man who stands out on the horizon of my memory like Mars at perihelion. When war broke out between Spain and the United States, it was very necessary to communicate quickly with the leader of the Insurgents. Garcia was somewhere in the mountain fastnesses of Cuba – no one knew where. No mail or telegraph could reach him. The President must secure his co-operation, and quickly.

What to do!

Someone said to the President, 'There is a fellow by the name of Rowan who will find Garcia for you, if anybody can.'

Rowan was sent for and given a letter to be delivered to Garcia…

[President] McKinley gave Rowan a letter to be delivered to Garcia; Rowan took the letter and did not ask, 'Where is he?'

By the Eternal! There is a man whose form should be cast in deathless bronze and the statue placed in every college of the land. It is not book-learning young men need, nor instruction about this or that, but a stiffening of the vertebrae which will cause them to be loyal to a trust, to act promptly, concentrate their energies: do the thing – 'Carry a message to Garcia...'"

Knowing is not enough. You have to do. We all have to do. Be like Rowan. Treat all of your tasks as "a message to Garcia." If you would like to have the full text of *A Message to Garcia*, go to http://BudBilanich.com/garcia.

I've enjoyed writing this book. It was fun to look back on my career and to distill the nuggets that have become my personal rules for success. But you should remember that these are ideas that I have found helpful in my personal journey to corporate career success. One size does not fit all. Change, adapt, discard ideas that don't work for you. Add new ideas that you find helpful or those you've learned in other places.

I have created a blog to accompany this book: www.blog.mycorporateclimb.com. Feel free to visit it. When you're there, please comment on any of the ideas in this book. Feel free to add ideas of your own or suggest modifications to what I've written.

This book and blog are a companion to my community of

success seekers – a membership site also called *My Corporate Climb*. It's a place where we freely exchange ideas and help one another learn, grow and succeed. You can join at http:// MyCorporateClimb.com. It takes more than one person to create a community. That's why I welcome your active participation on the blog. I will post there and respond to comments five days a week.

While I encourage open discussion of ideas on the blog, you can email me at Bud@BudBilanich.com if you have any questions you would like me to answer in private.

I am offering a free 30-minute coaching session to readers of *Climbing The Corporate Ladder*. If you are interested in taking me up on this, send me an email with your phone number along with a good time to call you.

Additional Books
By Bud Bilanich

Straight Talk For Success
*Common Sense Ideas That
Won't Let You Down*

42 Rules
To Jumpstart Your Professional Success

Your Success GPS

Star Power
*Common Sense Ideas
for Career and Success*

Success Tweets
140 Bits of Common Sense
Career Success Advice All
In 140 Characters or Less

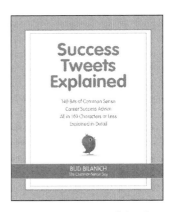

Success Tweets Explained
140 Bits of Common Sense Career Success
Advice All In 140 Characters or Less
Explained in Detail

4 Secrets of High
Performing Organizations
Beyond the Flavor of the Month
to Lasting Results

Using Values to Turn
Vision into Reality

Bud's books can be found at:

www.budbilanich.com/free-tips

www.amazon.com

Printed in Great Britain
by Amazon